BLOOD AT SAND CREEK

The Massacre Revisited

BLOOD AT SAND CREEK

The Massacre Revisited

Bob Scott

Cover art is Robert Lindneaux's version of Sand Creek,
Courtesy Colorado State Historical Society

Photograph of Bob Scott by Kolor Pro, McAllen, Texas

Cover design by Teresa Sales

The CAXTON PRINTERS, Ltd.
Caldwell, Idaho
1994

Library of Congress Cataloging-in-Publication Data

Scott, Robert, 1938–
    Blood at Sand Creek : the massacre revisited / by Bob Scott.
        p.   cm.
    Includes bibliographical references and index.
    ISBN 0-87004-361-7
    1. Sand Creek Massacre, Colo., 1854.   2. Cheyenne Indians--
Wars, 1864.   3. Cheyenne Indians--History--19th century--Sources.
4. Chivington, John M. (John Milton), 1821–1894.   5. United
States. Army. Colorado Cavalry Regiment, 3rd (1864)--History.
I. Title.
E83.863.S39   1994
973.7'37--dc20   94-15664

Lithographed and bound in the United States of America by
The CAXTON PRINTERS, Ltd.
Caldwell, ID 83605
158381

With grateful appreciation
for continuous encouragement from
Frank Kinsman, Dallas, Texas;
Stan Giles, Clinton, Iowa;
and to my family—
especially my son, Aaron Scott,
who has read and critiqued this story
at least a dozen times.

Contents

Illustrations

Preface

FIVE DAYS AFTER THANKSGIVING in 1864 several hundred US soldiers surrounded and attacked a Cheyenne Indian village on the banks of Sand Creek in extreme eastern Colorado. A fierce battle erupted, and when the shooting stopped a little more than seven hours later, a great number of Cheyennes—possibly as many as several hundred—and about a dozen soldiers lay dead or dying. The exact toll of human life was never established, and today remains one of the great controversies about the battle; estimates of Native American deaths range from just over 100 to more than 700.

It is known, however, that the majority of the Cheyenne victims—perhaps as many as two-thirds of the dead—were women and children or teenagers. The village was destroyed. One of the most famous of the Cheyenne chiefs, White Antelope, was dead; several lesser chiefs were also killed. Well-known Cheyenne chief Black Kettle survived the battle, although his wife was shot numerous times and critically wounded. Ironically, her life was saved by white doctors at Fort

Lyon—an action that of itself would become controversial.

The smoke would clear from the Sand Creek battlefield within minutes after the shooting stopped, but nearly everything else about the battle remains ensconced in haze and confusion, even after more than 100 years.

To this day, so-called facts reported about the Sand Creek confrontation are almost always incorrect. Worse than the inaccurate death toll figures are the inaccurate attributions of motives, which these modern reports suggest caused or contributed to the battle.

Many persons suggested in 1864—and many insist today—that the bloodshed at Sand Creek was the result of a deliberate attack on helpless and innocent women, children, and old men, instigated and led by a bloodthirsty politician who was seeking to enhance his reputation. Virtually all modern accounts of the battle portray the commander of the army troops at Sand Creek as a cold-blooded killer of innocents.

The Sand Creek Massacre ultimately ended both the military and political careers of that officer, a great US Civil War hero. Although it was not the first, the last, nor the bloodiest of the massacres of frontier Indians by white troops, Sand Creek became symbolic of the white man's mistreatment of Native Americans. It served as the springboard from which a new national conscience emerged; it remains today as the most often cited example of cruelty to Native Americans.

In truth, participants in much worse massacres— men such as Kit Carson, who was personally responsible for the starvation or freezing deaths of thousands of Navajos—somehow escaped the world's condemnation for their actions. Carson and others like him were allowed to testify against the soldiers who participated at Sand Creek. Carson personally testified at length against John Chivington, the commander who stood accused of knowingly permitting or eagerly leading the "unprovoked" Colorado attack. Carson was never challenged for his horrendous mistreatment of the Navajo people, and was portrayed in the Eastern press (and many subsequent history books) as a hero for speaking out against Colonel Chivington. Ironically, Carson and Chivington had been close friends and allies during the clash between Confederate and Union forces in New Mexico a mere two years earlier.

As recently as the middle 1970s, students at the University of Colorado railed against efforts to name one of their dormitories in honor of Civil War hero John Chivington, because Chivington was also the disgraced commander at the battle of Sand Creek. (The dormitory was eventually named something else.)

When the case of the Sand Creek incident had been thoroughly tried—not in a court of law, but in Eastern newspapers and the chambers of the United States Senate—John Chivington was forever disgraced. He was indelibly stamped as a heartless, cruel, Indian-hating bigot who took great personal pleasure in watching Native American women and children suffer and die. He was accused of personally murdering their babies and mutilating the bodies of their men, and laughing as he did so—although most of those charges clearly were dreamed up by New York newspaper writers or Chivington's political enemies in the Colorado Territory. His troops were pictured as drunken, brawling barroom trash, who laughed as they shot Indian babies or raped and murdered Indian women. (Tragically, some of those later charges may have been true, or at least partially true.)

Conversely, the tribal village at Sand Creek was portrayed as peace-loving and peace-seeking—Cheyennes who had given up fighting the white men and now sought only to live side-by-side with them in peace and harmony. Authoritative text and reference books today report this information as indisputable fact, as if there were no mitigating circumstances worthy of mention and no evidence to the contrary. Virtually without exception these modern texts indicate that the battle at Sand Creek was the result of an unprovoked attack by an undisciplined white mob, led by a bigoted and inept politician of questionable military ability. These are the same text books that virtually always portray the Native Americans in this instance as unarmed and peaceful.

The historian who carefully studies the history of the Frontier West finds it increasingly difficult to give credence to these modern accounts of the Sand Creek incident, even when the horrible treatment of the American Indian, in general, is considered. Modern text book versions of Sand Creek need examination in the light of hard evidence: evidence that many popular "historical facts" are wrong.

Questions about the accuracy of history arise when examining the character and personality John Chivington, the man who was vilified for his role at Sand Creek. Here is the larger-than-life hero who emerged as a great military leader, military genius, and—some people argue—possibly the savior of the Union, after crushing superior numbers of Confederate troops just two years earlier (see Robert Scott, *Glory, Glory, Glorieta.* Johnson Press, Boulder, CO, 1992).

The John Chivington of Glorieta Pass is portrayed as a brilliant, charismatic, dynamic, God-fearing frontiersman who chose to face overwhelming odds and probable death to defend truth and righteousness. The John Chivington of Sand Creek is seen as a bumbling, bloodthirsty coward who only fought against women and children—women and children who had surrendered.

Clearly, both of these portrayals cannot be right. Somewhere, somehow, either John Chivington or recorded history has gone awry. After spending more than a quarter century researching the John Chivington of Civil War fame, the author became convinced that the commonly accepted version of the tragedy at Sand Creek is at least tainted, if not downright inaccurate.

This book results from poring over all the available information on John Chivington, the military hero at Glorieta, and John Chivington, the villain at Sand Creek. Its conclusions come from twenty-seven years of combing historical documents, military records, newspaper accounts, text books, and other sources that recorded information about the tragic Indian Wars of the old West.

This book in no way seeks to excuse the years of cheating, murdering, and otherwise brutal mistreatment of Native Americans by frontier whites. It does not offer excuses for broken treaties, gun-running, land-grabbing or other crimes committed against American Indians. The book is not even an effort to cleanse the reputation of John Chivington, nor to place blame for an atrocity on some other pre-selected target. The author originally set out to simply try to understand the facts pertaining to the massacre at Sand Creek. The research indicates that the accepted version of not only this tragic battle, but the reasoning, motives, and actions of its participants simply are not true.

While the facts reported here may raise as many questions as they answer, they should at least change the perception of John Chivington and some of the other key players in this drama. That will please some people, and trouble others—especially those who are comfortable with history's apparently easy answers to our past. Whether you are among the latter or former type of reader, I hope you enjoy this book.

Bob Scott

BLOOD AT SAND CREEK

The Massacre Revisited

–ONE–

The Value of Life

AS THE SUMMER OF 1864 drew to a close, an epidemic of scurvy swept the isolated little army outpost of Fort Cottonwood, situated at the confluence of the North and South Platte Rivers in extreme southwestern Nebraska. Of the 124 men based at this strategic Oregon Trail crossing, more than half were ill with scurvy by the first of September. Physicians at the post had no medicine and few facilities to deal with the scurvy outbreak.

However, the doctors knew what to do; they had known for a hundred years that scurvy can be controlled by simply adding fresh fruit and vegetables to the diet. Unfortunately, in the absence of refrigeration an army outpost five days from the nearest town of any size was ill-equipped to stock the fresh foods necessary for a healthy diet.

The good news for the men of Fort Cottonwood was that a large grove of wild plum trees was located only a few miles south of the base. It was the season for the plums to be ripe, so the camp's doctor ordered all of the sick men, who were physically able, to travel to the grove and eat as many plums as they could handle. The trip would have two beneficial results; the sick men could enjoy the fresh healthy air of outdoors and could simultaneously fill themselves with the sweet wild plums, both of which would help them recover from the disease.

The morning of September 20, 1864, dawned bright and warm—one of those gloriously mild autumn days so frequent in the western part of the country. Indian summer, they called it, and it was one of most pleasant times of the year.

Captain Mitchell, in charge of "Operation Plum," ordered Corporal Anderson to round up a driver and bring an ambulance to the front door of the crude base hospital. Together they loaded seven weakened men into the ambulance—a flat-bed wagon with rolled-up canvas sides—and set off down the trail toward the grove of plum trees.

The roads on the frontier were in bad shape, and it took the better part of two hours for the ambulance to travel the seven miles between the fort and the grove. The length of the journey didn't matter to anyone; the sick men were enjoying the outing, and the officers were glad to get away from the boring routine of the army post.

Just before reaching the grove of plum trees the trail came off the high plateau and wound down through a shallow, narrow canyon about a mile in length. As the wagon-load of men rumbled into the open at the base of the canyon and entered the grove of plum trees, they met two soldiers from the base. These men were rounding up some horses that had wandered away from the base corral. Glad to have the company of the sick men, they dismounted and joined Captain Mitchell's group in picking plums.

The men had barely begun their pleasant task, when the serenity of the morning was shattered by the hard crack of a rifle. As the startled soldiers looked up, a group of about twenty Indian warriors emerged from a clump of trees, shooting at the soldiers as the braves walked toward them. What had been a pleasant outing suddenly became a mad confusion of frightened men, shouting and scrambling for cover.

The sick soldiers leaped back into the ambulance, as Captain Mitchell began returning the assailants' gunfire with his Colt revolver. When the soldiers were safely inside, Mitchell also leaped aboard, and the driver lashed the horses forward. The two soldiers who had recently joined the group jumped onto their own animals; one riding a horse, and the other a mule. The warriors mounted their horses, and a wild chase was underway.

As the wagon and animals began racing back up the canyon toward the fort, one of the mounted soldiers— the one riding the mule—was struck in the back by gunfire. He slumped forward in the saddle. After several seconds he slid from the animal, falling heavily to the ground. His pursuers were quickly upon him. One of the braves paused long enough to fire a rifle shot into the back of the soldier's head, then the warriors continued chasing the remaining soldiers.

The ambulance jolted wildly along the trail, the driver shouting something that was unintelligible in the noise and confusion of the gunfight. Captain Mitchell, firing out the rear of the ambulance at the pursuing Indians, turned and looked toward the front, trying to understand what the driver was saying. What he saw must have convinced Mitchell that all in his party were doomed. Thundering down the shallow canyon toward the ambulance were dozens of more warriors, waving weapons and shouting as they came.

Pointing up the side of the canyon, Mitchell indicated to the frightened driver to get the wagon to the top of the mesa, by going directly up the steeply sloped canyon wall. The captain hoped that if they succeeded in reaching the plateau, their attackers might be unable to surround the ambulance before the wagon reached Fort Cottonwood.

For a time it looked as if the maneuver might work. The assailants were taken by surprise when the wagon suddenly changed direction, and slowed their pursuit for several seconds. In a moment, though, they recovered from the surprise, and raced up the side of the canyon. They quickly cut the distance between themselves and the wagon-load of soldiers.

The wagon bounced and banged its way onto the higher and more level ground, and having reached the summit, continued its wild ride across the uneven prairie. Captain Mitchell and Corporal Anderson were still shooting out the back of the ambulance, and the remaining mounted soldier occasionally fired his revolver in the general direction of the pursuers. The gunshots all went wild, however. The shooting had no visible effect on the Indians, who continued to close the gap.

Soon the warriors were close enough to begin pouring a deadly rain of bullets and arrows into the ambulance. The assailants' arrows and bullets hit several of the sick soldiers. Some of the braves began galloping their ponies alongside the ambulance. They would hang off the opposite side of their horses and fire rifles from below the animals' necks. By holding on with one leg and arm, keeping their torsos on the other side of their animals, the braves presented almost no target at which the soldiers could shoot.

Eventually Captain Mitchell came to understand that continued flight was senseless. He concluded that the only hope for his beleaguered soldiers was to stop and make a stand. The captain was armed with one of the new Spencer repeating rifles, and two Colt revolvers. The corporal and teamster were each armed with repeating rifles, and the mounted soldier carried a revolver. Captain Mitchell reasoned that with so much firepower at their disposal, the soldiers might be able to hold the attackers at bay. At the same time, he hoped to make enough noise for someone at Fort Cottonwood to hear the gunfire and ride to their rescue.

Under the circumstances, the plan seemed like a good one. It might even have worked, had the wagon been stopped at once, while most of the warriors were still some distance behind. Unfortunately, by the time Captain Mitchell formulated his plan, both the ambulance driver and his horses were in a state of complete panic. Instead of trying to stop the animals, as ordered by Captain Mitchell, the frightened driver merely lashed them to an even greater fury. Recognizing the driver's panicky state, Captain Mitchell shouted to Corporal Anderson to climb onto the driver's seat, take over the reins, and stop the wagon.

But as Anderson tried to obey the command, the ambulance hit a deep rut in the prairie and bounced high into the air. The jolt caught Anderson off-balance, and catapulted him over the side of the wagon; he flew through the air and crashed to the ground in a battered heap. Captain Mitchell noted that the corporal managed to clutch his Spencer repeating rifle, even as he gathered himself and scurried for cover. Although bruised and breathless, Anderson scrambled into a small outcropping of rocks that offered him some limited protection from the enemy.

Captain Mitchell had little time to think about the unfortunate Corporal Anderson; the wagon was still wildly out of control, and the driver was still beating the horses. Handing his rifle to one of the sick men, Mitchell leaped forward to grab the reins and take control. Instead of reaching the seat, Mitchell met a fate identical to that of Corporal Anderson: as the captain scrambled toward the seat beside the terrified driver, the wagon hit another sizable ditch and bounced high into the air. Mitchell hurtled into the air, and ultimately to the ground.

Like Corporal Anderson, Captain Mitchell immediately scooted into a clump of nearby rocks and bushes. Unlike Anderson, however, Mitchell no longer had his repeating rifle; he had given it to a sick man before trying to reach the driver's seat. Mitchell found himself armed only with his two Colt revolvers.

The pursuing band of warriors saw Corporal Anderson being thrown from the wagon but—possibly because they were momentarily distracted—failed to see Captain Mitchell's fall. While most of them continued to chase the ambulance, about twenty others stopped and surrounded Corporal Anderson's hiding place. Captain Mitchell was perhaps 100 yards away— well out of pistol range—and could only watch helplessly as the attackers began closing in on the battered corporal.

Anderson was not an easy target, and was determined to fight to the end. When the warriors were within twenty yards or so of the corporal's position, he opened fire. Anderson was an excellent shot and made the most of his unfortunate opportunity. By the time he had emptied the seven-shot repeating rifle, seven of the enemy lay dead or dying. The corporal hastily reloaded and started shooting once again—killing two more with his next two shots.

Finally, however, the overwhelming numerical superiority of the assailants brought about the inevitable conclusion to the grim little battle; Anderson was wounded and fell forward. The attackers leaped to their feet and raced to the soldier's side. While Mitchell watched helplessly from his hiding place, they turned the wounded corporal face up, scalped him, and mutilated his body. Mitchell felt revulsion at the treatment of the body, but from all indications, Anderson died before the scalping occurred, and did not suffer through torture. For that, Mitchell was grateful.

Captain Mitchell was still uncertain whether any of the attackers had seen him fall from the ambulance, and whether the enemy would discover him, also. Mitchell crouched lower in his hiding place and waited, hardly daring to breathe.

Momentarily, the larger group, who had pursued the runaway ambulance, returned to the spot where corporal Anderson's body lay. They gleefully reported that they had overtaken the ambulance and the mounted rider, and had killed every man in the group. The returning braves proudly displayed the nine scalps they had taken.

For several minutes, the braves loaded the bodies of their dead companions on their horses. This not only allowed for proper burial of their heroes, but also kept the enemy from ever determining how successful he had been in battle. (It was a custom that would frustrate the army for nearly thirty years. The practice resulted in conflicting reports of the number of casualties in hundreds of battles.) After a brief period of excited chatter, the entire group rode away. They obviously were unaware of Captain Mitchell's presence.

Mitchell was afraid to leave his hiding place, for fear that stragglers might be in the area, or that the disappearance of the warriors was merely a trick to see if any other white men would appear. He stayed crouched in his cramped hiding place all day long— scarcely daring to move.

His muscles ached and his head throbbed from a lump he had taken when he hit the ground. Mitchell's legs were asleep and his knees ached terribly, but he was too afraid of discovery to change position, even a little bit. For more than six hours he endured the misery of his cramped hiding place, watching for any sign of the attackers.

It was well after dark before he finally crawled from the clump of bushes and began the long walk to Fort Cottonwood. He stumbled back inside the compound's protective walls at almost midnight, to report what immediately became known as the Cottonwood Massacre.[1]

The response to the massacre of the ten soldiers— seven of them too ill to put up much resistance—was immediate and widespread. The story, carried by newspapers throughout America and frontier West, demanded retaliation against the "savages." The debate even reached an outraged Congress, exerting great pressure on the army to retaliate. Ordinary citizens demanded that the government take steps to stop the attacks, and the government demanded action by the army. Busy fighting Confederates, the army could do little more than to issue orders to any units still operating in the West, to "pursue and punish hostile Indians." The Nebraska legislature passed a strongly worded resolution, condemning the Indians for this unprovoked attack.

Later historians would take a much broader, and much more conciliatory, view of the conflict between Native Americans and the pioneers and settlers. Typical of these accounts is the one written by three university professors in 1982:

> The Indians, of course, were reacting to the danger that the continuing immigration [of whites] posed to their lands and their way of life. In the 1851 Treaty of Fort Laramie, the United States had negotiated a general settlement with the Cheyenne, Arapaho, Sioux, Shoshoni and Crow tribes...The treaty confirmed the Southern Cheyennes and Arapahos in joint control of a vast territory lying between the trails to Oregon and Santa Fe. Embracing most of Great Plains Colorado, the southeastern corner of Wyoming, and parts of Nebraska and Kansas, it gave them the unbroken buffalo range between the North Platte and the Arkansas that they had used for two generations. Ten years later, in the Treaty of Fort Wise, the same tribes surrendered the bulk of their land under pressure from the United States government and from white settlers who had appropriated the heart of their hunting ground near the base of the mountains. Most of the leaders of the Arapahos and the peace chiefs of the Cheyennes led by White Antelope and Black Kettle supported the new agreement. Many of the younger men of the Cheyennes and the members of the warrior societies claimed that they had never agreed to the cession, and that the fraction of land north of the Arkansas retained by the tribes did not contain enough game to support their people. The record of the next two years shows occasional episodes of stealing livestock from government handouts.[2]

At the time, most settlers believed the Native Americans had received a fair settlement, and could not understand their reluctance to accept the proposed arrangements—even when the proposals were necessarily (in the white man's view) altered from time to time.

Perhaps what is more important, not everyone believed the Fort Cottonwood attack was unprovoked. Colonel William Collins, commander at Fort Laramie, suggested that the attack was probably the result of Confederate instigation. Confederate agitators, he said, were in the area, stirring up trouble and encouraging the Native Americans to attack white settlers. Colonel Collins may well have been right.

Notes

1. This is based on several accounts of the Cottonwood Massacre. One account of this incident was especially helpful; it is related in the book by Louis A. Holmes, *Fort McPherson, Fort Cottonwood* (Louis A. Holmes, Johnsen Publishing Company, Lincoln, Nebraska, 1963), 13–15.

    Some other accounts of this incident suggest that several of the soldiers in the ambulance survived the attack, but such information is not supported by official records. Evidence at the scene indicated that sixty to seventy Indians participated in the attack; it was widely believed they were Cheyennes.

2. Abbott, Leonard, & McComb, Colorado; *A History of the Centennial State,* (Colorado Associated University Press, Boulder, Colorado, 1982), 74.

–TWO–

Rebels in War Paint

MANY FACTORS led to the tragic Great Plains Indian wars—broken treaties, forced relocations, restrictions to hunting and trapping, pride, greed, inhuman conditions and inhumane treatment. In the middle of that protracted war—the middle 1860s—the two most obvious issues involved the Bureau of Indian Affairs, and a little-known and highly unusual Confederate strategy for winning the Civil War.

The Bureau of Indian Affairs—the BIA—was responsible for managing, controlling, and assisting the thousands of American Indians being displaced by the westward movement of white civilization. There were two fundamental problems in carrying out that responsibility. It put the BIA at cross-purposes with the rest of the American population, and the BIA was riddled with self-serving thieves who regularly cheated the Native Americans for their personal gain.

Problems inside the BIA were as old as the agency itself, and certainly predated the all-out wars that swept the plains like a summer prairie fire *circa* 1860–1870; it's just that everything else going on during the same era made the Indian problems more acute. Take, for example, the bitterly controversial BIA habit of supplying arms and ammunition to the Indians. The BIA regularly delivered modern weapons and plentiful ammunition to them, arguing that because the influx of white men had made hunting more difficult, the Indian people must have the modern weapons to kill enough game to avoid starvation. At the same time, the army and frontier civilians were regularly battling—literally for their lives—against thousands of hostile Indians, many (perhaps most) of whom were armed with these BIA-supplied hunting rifles.

This dispute placed the BIA in the middle of angry demands. The Indian people insisted that unless they had plenty of hunting weapons, they would have to fight to drive the white man from the area. The army and the settlers said it was these BIA rifles that permitted hostile factions to carry out their attacks against them.

Perhaps equally as bad was the fact that a huge percentage of the bureaucrats selected as BIA agents—the men charged with making certain the Indian people got what they needed—were themselves crooks. Many of these public servants looted from Indian storehouses, cheated the Native Americans on deals, virtually held them hostage—and then cried for army protection when the Indian people lashed out in retaliation. Thomas Galbraith, for example, was blamed almost entirely for causing the bloody Sioux uprising that swept Minnesota in 1862.

S. G. Colley was a distant (and unfriendly) cousin of Colorado Governor John Evans. Many people speculate that Colley's appointment was a BIA effort to appease the governor, with whom their relations had become seriously strained as a result of the arming-of-Indians issue.

Many historians accuse Colley of cheating the government and the Indians, lining his pockets with ill-gotten gains. There is strong circumstantial evidence to support those suppositions. Colley was a former army major with limited knowledge of Indian affairs. Some time later, he was accused of stealing their horses, and profiting from the illegal sale of whiskey to the people he was supposed to serve. Reputedly, he and his son became rich from such crooked dealings. However, Colley took office at a difficult time. Under the circumstances, it's hard to say how much of the problem between Native Americans and settlers resulted from Colley's actions, and how much was the result of other factors—such as Confederate meddling in white–Indian affairs.

The first shot had not yet been fired in the US Civil War when the South began making efforts to turn Indians against settlers in the West. The Southern strategy centered on two objectives, the most important of which was the capture the western one-third of the US for the Confederacy.

The Confederates correctly reasoned that once hostilities erupted, all of the US soldiers, then stationed at frontier outposts to protect the settlers, would disappear; many of them would go South to fight as Confederates, and the remainder to Washington to join the Army of the Potomac. That would leave the West naked and vulnerable to capture, should anyone be interested.

The South was very interested. Capture of this vast wilderness would assure the Confederacy of the two things it most desperately needed in order to fight the war—money and unblockaded sea ports.

The Confederates knew they would be desperately short of cash when the war started; the federal treasury was in Washington, DC, which clearly would remain in the hands of the Union. The South must find a way to come up with cash in order to buy arms, ammunition, and supplies with which to wage the war. That ready cash was clearly there for the taking in the largely unprotected gold fields of Colorado and California. In both of those places, gold rushes were in full swing; seizure of the gold would solve one of the two most pressing problems for the South.

The other Confederate concern was the need for deep sea ports, from which the South could carry on unrestricted commerce with Europe. Control of the west coast would solve the problem. The Union Navy would be able to blockade most or all Southern ports in the Atlantic and Gulf, but ports on the west coast could not be barricaded. To do so, the Union Navy would have to sail around South America and take positions in the Pacific; by the time they arrived on station they would be running short on supplies. Because Mexico was likely to side with the Confederates in the Civil War, the Union would have no place to get supplies.

There was a third, equally important, though less obvious goal for the Confederates in capturing the western United States; seizure of this huge territory would likely bring about formal diplomatic recognition of the Confederacy as a legitimate government. France, England, Spain, and Germany had all hinted that they were on the verge of giving such recognition, and needed only one major Confederate victory before doing so. Formal recognition would mean that the South could borrow money, buy military supplies on credit, and otherwise be in better position to fight and win the war.

There was one major flaw in this grand Confederate scheme; capture of the West would require personnel— even with almost no Union troops to resist such an invasion. Confederate soldiers would have to remain in control of key captured cities and outposts to prevent recapture by the Union, and the South could not spare troops for such a campaign any more easily than could the North.

The Confederates came up with what appeared to be a great solution to the problem; they would recruit Indian warriors to fight the Western battle for them. They reasoned that the Native Americans already disliked the white men, and could easily be persuaded to step up hostilities against them. Trained in modern military tactics and given modern military weapons, the braves almost certainly could overcome any resistance by local whites. To encourage the participation of tribal groups, the Confederates promised the Native Americans that, once the Civil War ended, the South would cede back to them all the territory from Kansas City to California.

The South began formally planning their Indian-aided Western invasion in 1860—nearly two years before Civil War hostilities erupted. To lead this unusual effort they eventually turned to Albert Pike, a 300-pound Arkansas lawyer who had successfully represented the Creek Indians in litigation against the Federal government—winning for them an $800,000 settlement of old claims. Pike was also a former newspaper reporter, school teacher, plantation foreman, scholar who spoke several languages, poet, and free thinker. Pike was also considered to be a little strange by those who knew him. He often pretended to be a Native American, and was "not above wearing Indian dress, appearing from time to time in leggings, moccasins, and even feathered headdresses of the plains Indians."[1]

Pike was named as the Confederate Commissioner of Indians. His orders were to begin recruiting, training, and arming Native Americans throughout the West, and helping them to plan attacks against whites. A number of Southern leaders—including the Arkansas Governor Henry Rector and Confederate General Ben McCulloch—had already met with the leaders of many western tribes, asking them to support the Confederacy. They told the Indian leaders that the North planned to invade and seize the Indian Nation (Oklahoma), and to forever drive them from the Great Plains. However, if they supported the South in the Civil War, the Confederates would fully support the Indian people in resisting such invasion—and would eventually give all of the Great Plains back to them.

These men, with the governor of Texas, told Confederate leaders they could recruit many thousands of Native Americans to fight against the Union. Commissioner Pike, now given the rank of General in the Confederate Army, was somewhat more pragmatic; he forecast a recruitment of 3,000–5,000 warriors. Pike had no illusions about the difficulty of controlling these recruits, whom he said would resist training and discipline.

Ultimately, he formally recruited fewer than 4,000 Native American men who fought in Confederate uniform, although he apparently was successful in arming hundreds or thousands of others to continue attacking Union soldiers and settlers throughout the West. This they did with great effectiveness.

There is reason to believe that Confederate agents actively armed and agitated tribal groups in Kansas, New Mexico, Colorado, Nebraska, Wyoming, and Utah. Nonetheless, documented evidence is limited to the formal treaties signed between the South and the five civilized tribes of Oklahoma. Friendly tribal groups in Colorado, however, told William Bent that Confederate agents actively negotiated with all the tribes of the Great Plains. According to these reports, the Confederates were delivering arms and ammunition, training Indian braves in modern warfare tactics, and promising great rewards to those who waged war against the white man.

There is at least a suggestion—never proven—that the Confederates supplied arms and ammunition to the Kiowas of Colorado. Several Kiowa tribes—especially those influenced by Chief Satanta—staged repeated attacks against Union wagon trains and army bases along the Santa Fe Trail. Those assaults may have been sheer coincidence, but the timing of offensive actions against key military installations seemed to indicate prior knowledge of troop movements: the sort of white-army tactics that were not normally a part of Kiowa war methods. In other words, the attacks seemed to have resulted from specific planning such as would have been encouraged by Confederate agents.

Colonel John Chivington, and the First and Second Colorado Volunteers, were locked in a deadly struggle with Southern troops in New Mexico in 1862. At least two wagon trains, bringing the Volunteers relief supplies, were destroyed by Kiowa attacks on the Santa Fe Trail. Historian Paul Wellman says the irritation caused by these constant assaults was largely responsible for the Sand Creek Massacre of Cheyennes, two years later—by troops under the command of Colonel Chivington.[2]

Without naming their sources, some other modern writers of history say that the Osage tribe agreed to help the Confederates fight the Union army and frontier whites, but that the Kiowa and Comanche tribes refused to participate. It is a fact that the Osages also agreed to help the Union; one group carried out certain assignments for the Union Army in Colorado. Several members of the tribe were hired by the commander of Fort Garland to intercept and "take care of" thirteen Confederate army recruiters riding into Colorado in late 1861. The Osage warriors did their job well; they returned to Fort Garland several weeks later carrying the heads of all thirteen Confederates in gunny sacks.

If the Confederates were restricted to merely agitating and encouraging hit-run attacks on the Great Plains, they were more successful in the formal recruiting of Native Americans in Oklahoma. Commissioner Pike's first actual recruiting effort began on Friday, March 7, 1862. He arrived near modern-day Oklahoma City with several wagon-loads of presents for the Cherokee, Creek, Chickasaw, Choctaw, and Seminole tribes. In subsequent meetings with tribal leaders, Pike promised to cancel all debts owed by the tribes to the United States Government, and promised they could have the Indian Nation (Oklahoma) forever if they would simply unite with the Confederacy to defend that territory from a Northern invasion. Pike's superiors had instructed him to promise the warriors that all they had to do to win permanent title to the land was merely to defend the area; he promised them they would never have to fight at any other location.

Pike found many of the tribal leaders receptive to his suggestion. Prior to the outbreak of Civil War hostilities, the local Indian Agent had been Douglas H. Cooper, a strong supporter of the Confederacy. Pike later credited Cooper with leading the Choctaw and Chickasaw tribes into the Confederate fold. Once those two tribes had agreed to help the South, the other three Oklahoma tribes quickly fell into line, in spite of a serious, continuing division among the Indian people as to whether they should fight for the North or the

South—or for themselves, as an independent third force. This ideological split eventually led to open warfare between the tribes, finally culminating on December 26, 1861; Troops numbering 1,400 men, of the Texas Third, Sixth, and Eleventh Cavalries, attacked and massacred hundreds of pro–Union Cherokees, including scores of women and children. The defeated survivors fled into Kansas, and eventually sought protection at local US Army outposts.

Pike had barely won agreement from the majority pro–Southern Native factions to aid the Confederacy, when his orders changed. Instead of defending the Indian Nation, Pike's warrior-soldiers were called to Arkansas, to battle an invading Union Army under General Samuel R. Curtis. Many Native Americans originally refused Pike's demand that they leave Oklahoma, citing the earlier Confederate promise that they would never have to fight outside their own territory. Pike was further hampered in trying to encourage his recruits to join the Arkansas battle because the Confederates failed to deliver additional wagon-loads of food, clothing, weapons, and supplies which had been promised to the tribes.

Nonetheless, Pike eventually led more than 3,000 braves into Arkansas in support of Confederate General Sterling Price. One of the deciding factors in convincing the warriors to go to Arkansas was an impassioned appeal made by Pike. He reminded them that the Union Army marching through Missouri was under the command of General Samuel Curtis, who was also in charge of those soldiers fighting other Native Americans across the Great Plains.

At the time Pike headed for Arkansas, Price's army was in full retreat from the advancing Union forces. Fortunately for Price, the Northerners had begun to run low on supplies, and finally halted their southward advance at the Missouri–Arkansas border. This halting of the Union invasion set the stage for the greatest confontation of the war between Union soldiers and Confederate Native American warriors.

General Samuel Curtis's Union Army force consisted of about 10,000 men. General Price's Confederate Army force consisted of 7,000 soldiers, but he was soon joined by General Ben McCulloch and another 8,000 men. In addition, General Pike soon showed up with about 3,000 braves, giving the Confederates a decided manpower advantage.

Early on the morning of March 7, the Confederate Army began moving northward, and soon encountered the Union troops dug in along Pea Ridge, Arkansas; the battle was immediately joined. In the opening minutes of fighting, General Pike ordered his Native American soldiers to charge a Union battery under the command of Colonel Peter J. Osterhaus. When they swooped out of the trees, giving their traditional war yelps, the startled Union soldiers briefly halted their shooting. The pause was just long enough to permit the warriors to sweep into the Union lines and engage the Northerners in bitter hand-to-hand fighting.

In a matter of seconds, Union resistance crumpled and the Northern soldiers were running for their lives. They regrouped a short distance away, however, when their enemies surprisingly failed to continue pursuit.

Pike was dismayed that the warriors did not chase the Yankees, but they apparently believed that simply capturing the Union cannons and forcing the Northerners to run for their lives was victory enough. The braves were now milling around the six captured Union guns as if the batteries had been the sole object of the conflict, whooping and shouting in triumph.

To the utter dismay of Pike and other Confederates, the warriors began to scalp the wounded and dead Union solders who lay near the captured batteries. To these warriors-turned-soldier, scalping was a natural part of combat; it had great religious and social significance. To the white men, the very thought was revolting, even if all the victims had been dead; the fact that the wounded survivors were also being scalped was absolutely appalling. In addition, several Union soldiers were apparently tortured, then slowly put to death by the warriors.

To make matters worse, no matter what Pike did he could not get the braves to quit their scalping, nor to stop the rest of their victory celebration. In fact, Pike couldn't even get their attention, and the Indian soldiers were soon completely out of control.

At the height of this wild battlefield celebration, one of the braves decided to set fire to an ammunition wagon sitting next to the cannons. Before anyone noticed what was happening, the flames swept into the gun powder and blew up. A number of celebrants were killed, and many others wounded by the blast.

At that precise moment, other Union cannons opened up on General Pike and his warriors. Dozens fell in the opening volleys of this strong Union counter attack, and the chanting and celebrating ended. Pike shouted at them to retreat, which they did—running full speed back to the Confederate lines. When Pike finally got his troops under control, he quickly marched them away from the battlefront.

Pike was so distraught at the uncivilized behavior of his soldier warriors that he subsequently sent a formal note of apology to Union General Curtis, assuring him that the Confederates did not condone the scalping, mutilating, or torturing of Union prisoners.

The note drew little attention, but the massacre of wounded Union survivors certainly did. Newspapers throughout the North screamed in outrage at the use of "hostiles" to torture and execute wounded Union soldiers. The incident caused a number of fence-sitting Missourians to join the Union cause, and was used as a rallying cry for the remainder of the War in the West. It also triggered outrage in Europe, and may have severely hampered continued Confederate efforts to win support and formal diplomatic recognition on the continent.

After Pike's warriors had been driven from the Union cannons at Pea Ridge, the full Union Army counter-attacked. In bitter fighting that followed, the North eventually was victorious. Pike and other Confederate forces fled south, and when the North chose not to push further into Arkansas, Southern regulars were soon diverted to other battlefields.

General Pike eventually took his regiment back to Oklahoma, angry and embittered because fellow Confederates treated both him and his warriors like second-class citizens. In addition, other Confederate troops had seized a supply of shoes, clothing, and weapons which had been ear-marked for Pike's men, and used the supplies for themselves; this further embittered Pike and his warriors.

The hostility of Confederate regulars against their Native American compatriots, and the bad press they generated at Pea Ridge, eventually doomed the formal Southern effort to recruit and use such troops on the battlefield. Nonetheless, those warriors already in uniform were committed to the cause, and would serve with distinction throughout the months and years that followed.[3]

Virtually unnoticed at the time of the Pea Ridge fighting (because it was of no particular significance to

Courtesy Colorado Historical Society

WILLIAM BENT, TRADER

Respected leader of the frontier West, Bent was married to a
Cheyenne woman and was trusted by both sides. He believed
whites usually mistreated Indians, and warned that Indians
were liars and killers. Bent fathered two sons who became
the most hostile Indian warriors in the West.

anyone at the moment) was the fact that one of the many Confederate soldiers who fought at Pea Ridge was a young private named George Bent. The Bent family would play a prominent role in later hostilities in western Kansas and Colorado. George was the half-breed son of Colorado's pro–Union fur trader, William Bent. The young Bent also fought in several more battles on behalf of the Confederates, finally suffering a minor wound in fighting at Corinth, Mississippi, on October 17, 1862. After that battle, Bent was rescued by a Union doctor who successfully treated the injuries. Bent was then confined to a prisoner-of-war camp and was later transferred to a prison near St. Louis.

As the captured Southerners were marched through St. Louis, an old family friend recognized Bent and raced to find his older brother, Robert Bent, who happened to be in town on business. Robert contacted influential family friends in St. Louis and quickly persuaded the Union Army to release George into the custody of his well-known father in Colorado. The Union had no objection to George's release; it meant one fewer Confederate prisoner to feed, and was seen as a sort of reward to Bent's loyal father.

The young Bent readily agreed to take a required oath, pledging that he would never again bear arms against the United States—and was set free. Bent would later argue that the vow he took in Missouri was not binding on him because of his Native American heritage.

At virtually the same moment, George Bent's younger brother Charles was being released from active duty by the Confederate Army. The reasons for his release are not certain; there is no record of his having been wounded or captured. Perhaps the Confederates released the younger Bent because of his age; he was barely sixteen years old when he volunteered for duty in the Southern army.

Charles Bent returned to Colorado within a few weeks of wounded George's return. Unlike George, Charles had not promised never to take up arms against the United States; in that regard he was slightly less deceptive than his brother when, a short time later, both boys began fighting US troops and civilians on the western frontier. Both were eventually deeply involved in the Sand Creek Massacre.

Although General Pike's regiment continued to fight through much of the Civil War, Pike himself turned his attention elsewhere. He and a number of his agents were rumored to be circulating among remaining tribes across the Great Plains. They spoke warmly of the great fame and rewards being earned by those warriors already fighting on behalf of the Confederacy. Plains Indians were constantly promised by these Confederate recruiters that if the South won the Civil War, the Confederates would give the Great Plains back to them forever, and would prohibit the white man from settling the land. These recruitment efforts were believed to have continued for the duration of the war, although little official documentation can be found to support that common supposition.

Shoshonis were said to have been armed and agitated by Southern agents to attack travelers in Utah in 1862. Colonel Patrick Connor, commander of Union troops in Utah, was completely convinced of the accuracy of reports linking trouble with tribal factions to what he called Confederate meddling, and ordered that since the Indian people were agents of the Confederacy, whenever they were caught, "...you are to immediately hang them and leave their bodies thus exposed as an example of what evil-doers might expect."[4]

Thursday, July 3, 1862. The Sixth Kansas Cavalry fought and overwhelmed Chief Watie's Confederate Cherokees in a vicious battle fought south of the Oklahoma–Kansas border. Many warriors were killed in the fighting, but Chief Watie and several hundred of his braves escaped from the battlefield.

On the same day, the Ninth Kansas Volunteers were joined by a battalion of pro–Union Indians who had been driven from Oklahoma because they refused to bear arms for the Confederates. Now known as the First Indian Home Guards, these warriors and the Kansas regulars defeated a small Confederate force at Locust Grove, near the Oklahoma–Kansas border. Following the battle, large numbers of Cherokees who had been fighting for the Confederates offered to switch sides and fight for the Union.[5] Their offer was not accepted, although they were encouraged to lay down their arms and return to the reservation in Oklahoma. Many of them apparently did so.

Thursday, September 30, 1862. General Thomas Hindman led a battalion of Native American volunteers against Union regulars at Newtonia, Missouri. The Confederate force was far larger than the Union's, and the North was quickly routed in the battle. The following day, after the Union had received reinforcements, the North returned to the battlefield and defeated the Southerners. As the Confederates fled from the battle, they ordered the Native American troops accompanying them to return to Oklahoma to defend their homeland against an anticipated invasion from the North.

Thursday, December 30, 1862. Union Colonel William A. Phillips led 1,200 Union soldiers, including about 200 members of the Indian Home Guards, in an attack against the Confederate-held Fort Gibson, Oklahoma. After a brief skirmish, the Southern forces fled into Texas. Northern troops chased the Confederates well inside the Lone Star State, burning crops and villages as they went; they finally abandoned the chase after penetrating more than thirty miles into Texas.

During the winter of 1862–63, and continuing well into the summer of 1863, tribal groups on opposite sides of the white man's war sporadically battled each other in Oklahoma. The overall results were inconclusive.

Wednesday, July 1, 1863. Elements of the Second Colorado Infantry, and the First and Second Kansas Infantry, were on the march through northeastern Oklahoma on their way to Arkansas when their supply train was attacked by a large Confederate force, which included several hundred Indians. The engagement, which was fought near Baiter Springs, Oklahoma, see-sawed for several hours before the tide of battle finally turned against the South, and the Confederates were forced to withdraw from the area.

Friday, July 17, 1863. A large Union force attacked a 5,000-man Confederate contingent at Honey Springs, Oklahoma. Again, several hundred warriors, under the leadership of General Albert Pike and Chief Stand Watie, were among the defenders. Although little is recorded of the fighting, it is known that the Confederates were eventually routed, and fled the battlefield in confusion.

Wednesday, June 15, 1864. Indian soldiers, under the command of Stand Watie, captured the Union supply ship *J.R. Williams* on the Arkansas River, and turned it over to the Confederates. Watie also seized an estimated $100,000-worth of Union supplies, which he also gave to the Southern command. In recognition of this feat, Watie was promoted to the rank of Brigadier General in the Grand Army of the Confederacy—the only Native American to hold such a high rank on either side of the Civil War.[6]

But the organized Cherokees, as visible as they were in Civil War battles, were not the only Native Americans recruited and used by the Confederates during the Civil War. One of the more curious—and tragic—of the battles involving warrior-soldiers occurred on Friday, April 15, 1864. Brigadier General Samuel B. Maxey led a division of Choctaws (and other Confederate troops) into battle at Poison Springs, Arkansas. The Southerners found themselves fighting against a division of Negro soldiers, and each side was infuriated at the troops being used by the other; Northerners were outraged to be battling Indians, Southerners irate at fighting blacks. When the Union was defeated in this fighting, both red and white Texans raced onto the battlefield and murdered wounded Union survivors. Later, both Texans and Indians were formally charged with the scalping of black Union victims.[7]

When the War finally began to wind down a few months later, it should not be surprising that it was the Indians—accustomed to fighting on the run—who would be the final Confederate soldiers to formally give up the struggle. Robert E. Lee gave up at Appomattox in April of 1865; General Simon Buckner surrendered the remaining Confederate regulars (to General Edward R. L. Canby, the commander of Colorado troops in the New

Mexico Campaign of 1862) on May 26, 1865. But General Stand Watie and his Confederate warrior-soldiers held out until June 23, when they finally surrendered at Doaksville, Oklahoma.

Amazingly, even with all of this open involvement in the Civil War, history has had little to say about Native Americans who fought in the war, or about the Southern strategy to recruit and train them to fight. Yet at the time the War was fought, most military commanders and political leaders of the West—Colorado, Wyoming, New Mexico, Kansas, and Nebraska primarily—were absolutely convinced that much of their trouble with the Indian people was the direct result of Confederate recruiting, training, arming, and agitating of Indian tribes.

As already noted, Colonel William Collins at Fort Laramie was among the first to speak openly of Confederate agitation of tribal groups in the West. He was followed soon thereafter by William Gilpin, the governor of Colorado, and by the commander of Colorado's home guard defense troops, Colonel John Chivington.

It was Chivington who uncovered hard evidence of Confederate involvement with Native Americans of the area. It was also Chivington who would lead the fight at Sand Creek.

Several weeks after the Sand Creek Massacre, hundreds of Southern Cheyennes and Arapahos (and possibly some Kiowa Apaches) attacked Julesburg, Colorado, and the nearby army outpost of Fort Sedgwick. The town was destroyed, scores of civilians and soldiers were killed in the fighting, and the fort was damaged beyond repair. During the fighting, the attackers used established Confederate military techniques, including using mirrors to signal battle commands—a white man's military tactic never before used by Indians—and employing standard Confederate attack formations. Some of the weapons recovered from the battlefield after the confrontation were Confederate-issued arms.

There seemed to be little question that these warriors had been trained and outfitted by Confederates.[8]

Notes

1. Alvin Josephy, *The Civil War in the American West* (Alfred A. Knopf, New York, 1991), 234–5.
2. Paul I. Wellman, *Death on the Prairie* (University of Nebraska Press, Lincoln/London, 1934), 96.
3. There are numerous accounts of the Battle of Pea Ridge, but the one offering the most detail on the use of Indian troops (and also appears among the most carefully researched) is found in Alvin Josephy's excellent book, *The Civil War in the American West*, 336-49.
4. *The Civil War in the American West* gives outstanding detail on various Indian warriors and campaigns during the Civil War. The information regarding Colonel Connor is on page 254.
5. Ibid., 356.
6. Ibid., 377.
7. Ibid., 212.
8. Among those reporting these facts is the respected book by David Berthrong, *The Southern Cheyennes,* (University of Oklahoma Press, 1975), 228. Perhaps the best and most detailed account of this battle, however, is found in "Indian Vengeance at Julesburg," the unpublished notes of Ruth Dunn, found in The Heritage Collection at the public library of Lincoln, Nebraska.

–THREE–

John Chivington

THERE COULD HARDLY HAVE BEEN a more unlikely frontier hero, with all of its macho implications, than John Milton Chivington. If a novelist had created Chivington, editors and publishers would have rejected him as being too improbable. Nothing about Chivington, save only his physical size, fits the image of the wild West. He didn't swear—or at least he almost never swore; he didn't drink at all; he was not a cowboy or a lawman, and until he was middle-aged, he never even carried a gun.

John Milton Chivington was a preacher. He was an ordained minister in the largest Protestant church in America, the Methodist-Episcopal Church with its more than three million members. But he was more than merely a minister, he was a respected church leader; a senior Elder who began to have a tremendous impact on the church very early in his career.

Chivington was an ardently religious man in the genre of preacher caricatures; he was extremely conservative and essentially humorless. He took his church work as seriously as he took the Bible; it was holy, and it was beyond reproach.

By the middle 1840s, Chivington was prominent in church affairs. He was responsible for Sunday School development and for church planting in the heartland of America, the Midwest. More than that, he had become one of the country's most outspoken churchmen on the issue that was beginning to polarize America: slavery. Chivington ardently believed that slavery was a great sin, and that no man who possessed slaves would end up in heaven.

The first recorded instance in which Chivington faced pro–slavery elements occurred at a small local church in Ohio. The story goes that Chivington had decided to preach a series of fiery sermons on the evils of slavery.

After his first sermon, several men in the congregation approached Pastor Chivington and told him that not only were they in favor of slavery, but that they felt so strongly about it they would not tolerate another sermon on the subject. The men warned the preacher that if he ever again spoke against slavery, they would tar and feather him, and run him out of town on a rail.

The following Sunday morning there was an air of expectation when the church service started. The town was small, and everyone knew of the threat upon Chivington, should he continue his plan to preach on slavery. All eyes were on the preacher as he strode to the dais.

Chivington was dressed all in black, in keeping with the custom of the day. He calmly laid a large Bible on the podium and made a show of opening it and finding a particular passage. Then, without looking up, Chivington unbuttoned his suit coat and pulled back the sides; beneath the coat he was wearing a gun belt with two pearl-handled Colt revolvers.

The preacher quietly pulled the pistols and laid one on either side of the Bible. Then glancing up at the congregation for the first time, he began preaching on the evils of slavery. Not a word of protest was heard— during or after the sermon.[1]

That incident propelled Chivington into the church spotlight and into the undisputed leadership role of the most conservative wing of the denomination. And it set the stage for a debate that ultimately destroyed the Methodist-Episcopal organization. When the congregation's leadership met in their national convention in 1848, the church was braced for a major debate on slavery. The problem was that the president of the group was a Southerner and a slave owner. Chivington's faction demanded that he either sell his slaves or resign his post; he would do neither.

The result was a three-way split in the church: the pro–slavery element in the South, the anti–slavery element in the North, and a small neutral branch along the Mason–Dixon line. Although churches would be founded under the banner of the Methodist-Episcopal leadership for another twenty years, the church actually ceased to function as a national organization at the 1848 convention.

Ten years after the convention, Chivington was still opening new churches and organizing Sunday Schools for the most conservative branch of the Methodist-Episcopal denomination. By coincidence or by design, his church-planting nearly always took place at the western edge of the rapidly expanding frontier. He moved from Ohio to Illinois, then to Missouri and to Nebraska, and eventually was sent to Denver in an effort to bring Christianity to the thousands of would be gold miners flocking to Colorado after gold was discovered on Little Dry Creek near Denver in 1859.

The impact of the gold discovery on white–Indian relations can hardly be over estimated. Prior to the finding of gold, white men were mostly just an annoyance to Great Plains Indians, with a few actual gun battles thrown in from time to time. True, there had been conflicts for nearly thirty years, but the serious confrontations were nearly always isolated incidents. In more cases than not, the whites in Colorado prior to the gold discovery in 1858 were fur traders who were doing business with—and frequently living with—Indians. But when gold was discovered, the occasional white man suddenly became an explosion of white emigration.

As soon as gold was found on Little Dry Creek and on nearby Cherry Creek four days later, Eastern newspapers carried huge front-page stories about the fabulous gold discoveries. By June 1 of that year, about 150 prospectors were camped along the two creeks. By the middle of July—just six weeks later—the number of prospectors had soared to about 1,000. By the end of the summer, more than 100,000 would-be miners were crammed along the river banks in what is now Denver.[2]

This huge influx of settlers was far greater than anything anyone had ever anticipated—especially the Indian. Local tribal leaders were dismayed and alarmed at the arrival of so many whites, and the impact was felt especially by the southern Cheyennes and Arapahos, who lived and hunted in the general Denver area. In August, several of the chiefs pleaded with the Bureau of Indian Affairs to create a new treaty that would protect their interests. The Bureau promised to look into the matter, but with typical bureaucratic paralysis, did very little to implement any new plan.

Perhaps not everyone was really surprised by what was happening. Colorado's senior citizen, fur trader William Bent, was quoted in a Saint Louis newspaper as saying the Indians had feared a Colorado gold rush for many years. A reporter for the Journal of Commerce quoted Bent as saying that Indians had known about Colorado's gold for many years. He said a chief once told him that if the white man ever found the gold, they would take from the Indian "their best and last home."[3]

For the Indian, the issue was not possession of the gold; the Native Americans had little interest in the sparkling rock and did not care if someone else possessed the ore. The issue was not ownership of the land, either; the Indians had no concept of land ownership as practiced by white men. To them, everyone owned the land and shared in it equally. The problem was that the huge influx of settlers, brought to Colorado by the discovery of gold, would destroy Native American hunting grounds and frighten the buffalo herds that were absolutely essential to their survival. The Indian complaint was completely valid but, for the most part, fell on deaf ears.

The gold rush presented a great opportunity for John Chivington to expand his conservative church. What place needed religion more than a gold camp? Chivington apparently arrived in Denver early in 1860, and quickly became a popular circuit rider, bringing his preaching to gold camps that had begun to spring up along scores of mountain streams west of Denver.

Chivington immediately stood out in the crowd of rough-and-tumble miners. While most men in the territory were slovenly, unshaven, crude, hard-drinking, hard-swearing, and hard-fighting, Chivington was a gentleman. In addition, he was much bigger than the other men; Chivington stood about 6' 2", and weighed

220 pounds. He was a barrel-chested man who looked like he could hold his own in a brawl if it ever became necessary to do so, but Chivington was refined and well educated, with a postgraduate degree in theology.

In a short time, Chivington was just naturally recognized as one of the leaders of Denver and the new Colorado Territory, which had only recently been carved out the western half of Kansas. He became the friend and confidant of the appointed political leaders, including Governor William Gilpin.

In 1861, Governor Gilpin became aware that Confederate sympathizers were hard at work in Colorado, trying to recruit Indians to battle the local white population. Worse, Gilpin learned that the Confederates were planning an invasion of Colorado, in an effort to seize the territory's gold mines. Gilpin tried repeatedly to get help from the US Government to stop the Confederates, but his pleas were ignored.[4]

Gilpin eventually decided that if the Confederates were to be stopped, he would have to do it himself, without federal help. So Gilpin began organizing his own Colorado army. He offered the position of chaplain to his friend, John Chivington, and was surprised at Chivington's response. The big preacher declined to be chaplain, saying if there were battles to be fought he wanted to go as a soldier. Chivington believed that Jefferson Davis was the personification of evil, Satan himself, and wanted an opportunity to strike a blow for Christianity and prohibitionists.

Chivington turned out to be a great soldier and a natural leader of men. Commissioned a major, he soon became the de facto leader of the First and Second Colorado Volunteers. Eventually he was promoted to the rank of Colonel, and was made the actual leader of the troops. Under Chivington's command, the Colorado

Courtesy Colorado Historical Society

COLONEL JOHN M. CHIVINGTON

Commander of the Third Colorado Volunteers, hero of the Civil War, a man of proven courage: he was also dogmatic and unbending. Was he a cold-blooded coward, as well—who delighted in murdering helpless women and children? Evidence shows that history may have judged him inaccurately.

Volunteers performed amazingly well. Outnumbered more than four-to-one by an invading Confederate Army, the Coloradans and a handful of New Mexico volunteers crushed the Confederates and drove them from the West. The victory was assured when a Chivington-led group of 400 soldiers got behind enemy lines and completely destroyed the main Confederate base camp, including scores of wagons filled with arms, ammunition, and supplies needed for the campaign to capture Colorado and the remainder of the West.

When Chivington returned to Colorado in 1863, no one questioned his right to be the commander of the territory's military forces. In fact, few people questioned his right to do anything he wanted to do; he was a legitimate national hero who had saved Colorado and the remainder of the West from Confederate invasion. The newly organized Republican party began grooming Chivington for a run at the congressional seat that would be available as soon as Congress granted statehood. That alliance with the GOP brought Chivington his first powerful enemies in the territory. It was probably the first step toward his eventual downfall.

At about the time Chivington became active in Colorado politics, the territory began assigning political boundaries to what would eventually become counties. The mere division of this territory was a violation of the Treaty of Fort Laramie, which promised the Native Americans that Colorado would never be subdivided into white man's political units. If the white men noticed this violation, they apparently didn't care.

Had Governor Gilpin and Colonel Chivington (and other Colorado leaders) not been so swept up in the gold rush and the huge influx of whites, they might have paid more attention to a warning sounded by the wise old trapper, William Bent. He reported that leaders of the Cheyenne and Arapaho tribes were greatly alarmed by the continued migration of whites, the growth of white cities, the fencing of land, and the wagons that frightened the buffalo herds. Bent sent letters to Governor Gilpin and to the Bureau of Indian affairs (BIA), saying the Native Americans were "restless and bewildered;" he warned that failure to heed the Indians' complaint could lead to far more serious consequences.[5]

And Bent, who had a way of seeing the big picture, went even further in his warning. As a result of the rapidly growing the white population, an alarming split had developed, and was widening rapidly among the Indians; a split that was not tribe to tribe, but rather a difference between young and old: a serious generation gap.

The older Indians wanted peace with the white man. They wanted to learn to become farmers and to carry on commerce with their white neighbors.

The young Indians wanted war, and a return to the old way of life before the white men came to this territory. They were prepared to do whatever it took to drive the white man back to the east.

Bent's letter to the BIA warned that serious trouble was unavoidable unless something was done quickly to stop gold prospectors from laying claim to land already assigned by treaty to the Indians as their hunting grounds. Cheyennes, in particular, were angry and ready to fight—if it would stop whites from crossing the Smoky Hill Country along the Kansas-Colorado border, or otherwise interfering with their hunting.

But it was already too late to stop the growing pressure for an all-out war. Confederate agitators continued to stir up the tribes in Colorado, and the mere presence of white settlers continued to anger the Indian population. White men ignored old treaties, and flocked into the region—usually with the government's blessing and assistance.

The extent to which the white man ignored the signs of trouble is evidenced by the letter that Iowa Congressman Samuel R. Curtis wrote to the governor of Kansas. Curtis said that steps ought to be taken at once to move the Indian people off Colorado land where prospectors wanted to pan for gold. The Congressman said that some way should be found to compensate the Indians for the land, but they must be moved because the land is "of far more significance to the whites than to the Indians." He failed to mention that his son was already in Denver, panning for gold. (It is ironic that Curtis would author such a letter; he later became General Curtis, and was charged with the responsibility of fighting these same Colorado tribes at the height of the long Indian war.)

With the nation concentrating on the Civil War, which was then at its apex, few had time to think or worry about upsetting a few Indians in the West. New York newspaperman Horace Greeley visited Auraria (Denver) during this time frame, and thought that the Indian people had to bear the full responsibility for trouble in the West. Greeley wrote that his several visits to the West convinced him that Indians were instinctive thieves.[6] This sort of publicity made normal relationships between the two groups nearly impossible, even if everything else had been going well.

Notes

1. This story about John Chivington is told in nearly all histories, although there is little documentation for it. One particular version of the story is told in the book by Duane Shultz *Month*

of the Freezing Moon; (Martin's Press, New York, 1990), 5.

2. David Lavender, *Bent's Fort* (University of Nebraska Press, Lincoln/London, 1972), 358.
3. Ibid., 359.
4. For details, see Robert Scott, *Glory, Glory, Glorieta* (Johnson Press, Boulder, Colorado, 1992)
5. Bent's Fort, 361–2.
6. David Berthrong, *The Southern Cheyennes* (University of Oklahoma Press, 1975), 145.

–FOUR–

The Trouble in Colorado

INDIAN TROUBLE was not a new phenomenon in the
western part of the country; there had been sporadic
fighting here since at least 1833, when the earliest
fur trappers and explorers headed west. But since the
Confederates began agitating Indians in 1860 and since
the Colorado gold rush really got going in 1859, the
clashes between Native Americans and the white
newcomers had grown steadily and alarmingly in both
number and seriousness.

Trouble became especially severe after the vast
majority of soldiers pulled out of the frontier with the
onset of the Civil War. Since there were almost no troops
remaining anywhere west of Kansas City, warring tribal
factions seemed to grow increasingly daring and brazen
in their battles with white settlers. And the trouble
intensified after the bloody uprising in Minnesota in
1862.

During this time of mounting tension between the
Indian and the white man, there began to develop a
small number of elite super warriors, a sort of Indian
equivalent to modern-day special forces. The men of

these groups were the toughest and best fighters of the tribe, and were treated with extra honor and respect. Their only responsibility was to wage war and protect the tribe from enemies.

Among the plains Indians, these soldier societies were known variously as the Coyote Warriors, Flint Warriors, Fox Warriors, Crooked Lances, and—the most deadly and feared of all—the Dog Soldiers.

> [The Dog Soldiers were] the fiercest and most daring of all the Cheyenne warriors in the '60s and '70s. The name is a translation of the Cheyenne name for "the fraternity," the Ho-ta-min-tanio. It had organizations not only among the Cheyennes, but among the Sioux, Arapaho and other plains tribes. It had its own dances, songs, ceremonial costumes and insignia, besides special medicines and taboos.[1]

Although the Dog Soldier society was originally led by a Cheyenne chief named Tall Bull, the leadership role was soon assumed by a huge and fierce Southern Cheyenne warrior, known as Roman Nose. By the middle of 1862 (while Colonel John Chivington was still in New Mexico, protecting the territory from which he had just driven the last of the Confederate invaders), Roman Nose and his warriors were terrorizing eastern Colorado and western Kansas.

The factors contributing to the Indian unrest—the growing number of whites in Indian territory, Confederate efforts to stir up trouble, and white men making and breaking treaties—got one additional element in 1863 and 1864: a severe drought. Grasslands dried up. These grasslands normally supported the huge buffalo herds on which the Indians relied for meat, clothing, material for tents, and many other items. As a result, the buffalo herds migrated far to the north—to the Dakotas—in search of food and water, leaving thousands of Indians on the brink of starvation. Western settlers also worried about starvation, both because of the drought and because of the continued Indian raids against supply trains heading to Denver from Kansas City. The little food available was carefully guarded and hoarded, increasing the tension even further.

By January of 1864, the Indians of Colorado were desperate for food. They flocked to trading posts, such as Bent's Fort, exchanging everything of value for anything they could eat. Given the history of the frontier, it is not surprising that unscrupulous white traders took advantage of the situation: paying lower and lower prices for buffalo robes and other items being traded in desperation by the Indians. As the situation became a full-blown crisis, many Native Americans turned to whiskey for consolation. Naturally, these unscrupulous traders had much whiskey available for trading, sometimes literally exchanging a bottle of watered down whiskey for the robe off the back of an Indian.[2]

Colorado BIA agent H. T. Ketcham, dismayed at what was going on, wrote to Washington about it. His report cited "a shocking amount of dissipation, licentiousness, and venereal disease among Indians on the Arkansas River." He said white traders encouraged Indians to steal livestock from ranches, then trade the stolen animals for more whiskey. Ketcham claimed that traders entered Indian villages day and night with their loads of whiskey, and that prostitution among the women of the tribe had become a major problem for the increasingly frantic Indian people.[3]

Indian Agent Colley, assigned to the Arkansas valley, thought the drought was a golden opportunity to convert Cheyennes and Arapahos to the life of farmers rather than hunters, and encourage peace at the same time. He began moving full speed to implement such a program that, ironically, the Indians themselves had been requesting for at least fifteen years. Colley said he planned to hire Mexican field workers who understood farming, and have them train the Indians on planting and harvesting corn and other crops. Even in his enthusiasm for the plan, Colley noted that only the older members of the tribe seemed willing to learn to be farmers. Younger braves remained openly hostile to the idea in spite of the food shortages, and openly talked of waging war against whites.

Colley, Ketcham, and other BIA agents felt it was imperative that the Indian people view the BIA as an agency concerned only with their welfare. In pursuing that image, the BIA increasingly found itself on opposite sides of the fence from the US Army and local government officials.

BIA agents throughout the West lobbied constantly for the government to supply Indians with modern arms and ammunition. Colley and other agents believed that, because of the drought, it was more imperative than ever that the Indian people be able to hunt successfully: something they could do only if adequately armed. Since the white man was at least partially to blame for the buffalo shortage—wagon trains frightened the animals away from the traditional hunting grounds—the white man should help compensate for the problem. The BIA agreed with the recommendations and, in spite of strong opposition from the government of Colorado and the US Army, began shipping quantities of modern weapons and ammunition to the Indians.

Friday, March 25, 1864. The Confederate Army launched a major new northward offensive into Missouri, and appeared ready to also invade Oklahoma from Texas. General Samuel R. Curtis, commanding officer, was ordered to send every man he could round up to resist this new Southern attack. Curtis ordered the pullout of about eighty-five percent of all soldiers stationed in Colorado, Kansas, Wyoming, and Nebraska. On Saturday, March 26, Curtis telegraphed Colorado Governor Evans, warning that henceforth Colorado would have to supply its own troops for defense against Indian attacks; federal troops were no longer available for frontier duty.

Three days later, Governor Evans received more bad news. A letter from BIA agent Colley told of overwhelming new evidence that the Cheyennes, Arapahos, and Sioux intended to attack every white man between Kansas City and Denver in the months ahead. He advised Evans that intertribal hostilities seemed to be increasing, as well.

About March 1, a raiding party of Cheyenne and Arapaho warriors had attacked a Ute village in the mountains west of Pueblo, stealing around sixty horses. They apparently needed the animals to carry out a planned spring campaign against white settlers. Ute warriors chased the Cheyenne and Arapaho raiders well out onto the plains of eastern Colorado. They eventually surrounded the Cheyenne raiding party, recaptured all the horses and, according to reports reaching Bent's Fort, killed a substantial number of Cheyennes and Arapahos.

Agent Colley reported rumors that Arapaho and Kiowa warriors also had gone to the Texas panhandle to steal horses for another campaign against the whites. Later, however, only Kiowa warriors returned from the raid, leading the Arapahos to conclude that the Kiowas had double-crossed and murdered the Arapahos. Colley said he believed a war between those two tribes was imminent, and warned that "if war begins, it will sweep the plains and cannot avoid involving every white man in the territory."[4]

When at last the Union had enough spare soldiers to relieve the Colorado volunteers in New Mexico, Colonel Chivington returned to Colorado near the end of 1863. Governor John Evans immediately summoned him to his office. Chivington had repeatedly volunteered for duty on the Civil War battlefronts in the East, but was told instead that he should return home to Denver and head up the defense of Colorado. Governor Evans was desperate for military help. Almost every a day new reports came of Indian atrocities on the eastern plains of Colorado. Rightly or wrongly, most of the trouble was attributed to Roman Nose and his Dog Soldiers.

By the time spring weather arrived in 1864, the conflict between whites and Indians in Colorado had reached massive proportions.

Thursday, April 7, 1864. General Curtis received word that raiders had attacked the ranch of Irwin and Jackman and Company—a firm that supplied animals to the US Army. The report said Indian warriors had cut fences and stolen 175 beef cattle; some of the ranchers said they saw them driving the cattle away. General Curtis telegraphed General Mitchell at Omaha, telling him the stolen steers must be recaptured at all costs. General Mitchell, in turn, passed the buck to Colonel William O. Collins, commander at Fort Laramie, Wyoming. Collins' orders were to "recapture the stock and punish the scoundrels involved."[5]

Colonel Collins was one of the calmer influences on the frontier. Described as a tall, black-bearded lawyer, Collins was a former member of the Ohio State Legislature. Western author and researcher Alvin

Josephy quotes an unnamed fellow officer as saying Colonel Collins was levelheaded and an unbigoted man, determined that everyone should get a fair break. Captain Lot Smith said of Collins:

> [The colonel] is decidedly against killing Indians indiscriminately and will not take any general measures, save on the defensive, until he can ascertain satisfactorily by whom the depredations have been committed, and then not resort to killing until he is satisfied that peaceable measures have failed.[6]

Unfortunately, Colonel Collins was too desperately short of personnel to be tracking down cattle thieves—so he, too, passed the buck. Collins telegraphed Colonel Chivington and Governor Evans in Denver, asking for Colorado troops to pursue the thieves. He mentioned that Chivington was free to use any federal soldiers who remained in the territory, if that would help achieve the purpose. Collins specifically told Chivington that the army felt it was very important to recover the cattle so that the Indians would know they could not steal from soldiers.

Collins' telegraph told Chivington he should "not let any district lines prevent pursuing and punishing guilty Indians."[7] Colonel Chivington quickly dispatched regular army Lieutenant George S. Eayre, fifty-four men, and two mountain howitzers to try to locate the missing cattle. Chivington passed along to Eayre the specific instructions from Colonel Collins. Army orders were to punish those involved in the theft.

Tuesday, April 19, 1864. Just as Eayre was getting underway to search for the cattle thieves in eastern Colorado, a large band of braves attacked a ranch near

Courtesy Colorado Historical Society

MAJOR JOSEPH DOWNING

A Civil War hero and close Chivington friend, he was a no-
nonsense Indian fighter of the regular army. He thought
Chivington was too soft on Indians, and believed all Indians
had to be killed in order for whites to survive.

Julesburg in extreme northeastern Colorado. The ranch family fled safely, but the raiders ransacked the house and stole all available cattle and horses. The rancher and elements of the US Army sent to investigate the attack agreed that those involved were Cheyennes, most likely Dog Soldiers.

Army Major Jacob (or Joseph) Downing, a veteran of the Second Colorado Volunteers, had fought brilliantly in New Mexico. Colonel Chivington sent Downing to the scene of the attack to track and recover any of the stolen animals. A short time later, Downing telegraphed a message to: there were so many hostile Indians in the area, he hardly knew which way to turn. He urgently requested troop reinforcements.

Downing's telegram, sent to both Governor Evans and Colonel Chivington, said that ranchers were abandoning all ranches and settlements throughout the northeastern quarter of the Colorado Territory. He warned that unless the Indian raids stopped, immigration would cease and Colorado would become unfit for (white) habitation.

Major Downing reported that the evidence at the scene of the latest attacks clearly proved Cheyennes, possibly assisted by Kiowas, to be involved in the raids. Downing suggested that a large military detachment search for the main hostile encampment in the area, ride in and demand a halt to the raids, the return of all animals, and "if they refuse, wipe out the bunch of them!"[8]

On April 9, Lieutenant Eayre picked up the trail of the stolen army herd along Sand Creek, not far from Fort Lyon. A spring snowstorm delayed the pursuit several days, but on April 14, Eayre's scouts again picked up a distinct trail heading toward the northwest. The trail, made by a large number of cattle and several unshod horses, led directly into a small Cheyenne camp consisting of five tepees. Warriors in the village spotted the troops coming and fled from the area before the soldiers arrived.

One brave, possibly a rear guard scout, was spotted and chased by two of Lieutenant Eayre's men a short time later. The Indian managed to escape after shooting and wounding one of the soldiers. The soldiers said they did not fire on the Indian. Angered by the wounding of a man in his command, Eayre pushed his men even harder to catch the cattle thieves.

Tuesday, April 19. Lieutenant Eayre came upon a sizable Cheyenne village, but found it to be abandoned. In their haste to get away from the soldiers, the Indians left behind all of their belongings, including nineteen steers. All of the cattle bore the brand of the US Army. Under orders to punish the Indians, Lieutenant Eayre burned their village to the ground.

Later, Indians from the village claimed they had been hiding nearby and could have overwhelmed Eayre's soldiers and killed all of them at that moment, and were prepared to do so. According to these reports, they chose not to attack because Cheyenne Chief Black Kettle warned them that such an attack would only bring greater trouble to the Indians. Since this story was not made public until a year later (during the time the army was investigating Colonel Chivington and soldiers under his command) there is some question as to whether it is accurate.

Monday, April 25, 1864. Indian raiders attacked an Overland stage relay station just west of Julesburg. They set fire to the buildings and ran off about seventy horses. Soldiers sent to the scene trailed the horses to a recently abandoned Cheyenne camp, and burned several still-standing tepees. Major Jacob Downing, who led the raid, reported that his horses were so exhausted from constantly chasing Indians, they had no stamina to pursue this particular group any further.

The dispatches exchanged between troops in the field and the government, or military headquarters in Denver, clearly demonstrated growing frustration and impatience. No one was doing much talking about the causes of the unrest— only the fact that the unrest had to stop.

Wednesday, April 27, 1864. Major Downing and forty of his men rode over a ridge and found a young Indian brave alone in the middle of a grassy meadow. They captured the warrior, who was half Cheyenne and half Sioux. Major Downing was in no mood for idle conversation; he apparently assumed any Indian found in the area was bound to be hostile. Reports later filed with the army said that Downing threatened to shoot the teenager on the spot unless he supplied accurate information to the troops. There is some question whether the threat was anything other than a bluff, although summary executions of Indians by whites and whites by Indians were common at the time.

The army report says the young warrior pleaded for his life, and offered to lead the soldiers to the camp of those who had carried out a series of raids in the area. He promised that the army would find many of the stolen animals in this particular camp.[9]

Downing agreed to spare his life, and the brave led the soldiers sixty miles to the northeast, just inside Nebraska Territory. Shortly before dawn on May 3, the Colorado troops surrounded a sizable Indian village; the Indians in camp were still sound asleep. Downing sent ten men to seize the herd of Indian ponies, and detailed five others to hold the army horses. Then Major Downing and his twenty-five remaining soldiers attacked the Indian village.

About eighty warriors and an undetermined number of women and children fled into a rocky canyon at the back of the village, and a violent battle erupted. Soldiers later said that the Indian women and children took up weapons and were shooting at the soldiers, or helping to load the firearms for warriors. Major Downing was unable to advance against the fierce resistance, and at dark he ordered his troops to withdraw. The Indians also took advantage of the darkness to flee from the area in the opposite direction.

The following morning, Downing returned to the village, where he reported finding the bodies of twenty-five Cheyenne warriors. He estimated that thirty to forty more braves were wounded in the fighting, but had managed to escape. Downing's formal report claimed there were no casualties among the women and children—a report that is difficult to believe if they were really standing beside braves during the battle. Downing reported taking no prisoners, but said he recovered about 100 horses, many identifiable as stolen from ranches in the area.

In his formal report on the battle, Downing noted that if he had more men, or if he had some mountain howitzers, he could have wiped out the hostile Indians. The major went out of his way to praise Lieutenant Clark Dunn for his bravery during the battle, in the face of "strongly superior enemy forces." Downing closed his narration by warning "I believe this incident is the commencement" of an all-out war with the Cheyennes and other Indians in the (Colorado) region.[10]

Over the next five days, reports of Indian attacks came in from all sections of eastern Colorado and western Kansas. Wagon trains were burned, people accompanying the wagons killed or kidnapped, and the animals stolen. A number of ranches were also burned. The attacks never involved fighting between soldiers and Indians; the warriors avoided confrontation with soldiers and attacked only small groups of unarmed or lightly armed civilians. They left few survivors.

Sunday, May 1, 1864. With Indian raids increasing in both number and severity throughout the eastern half of Colorado, Governor Evans was facing increasingly great pressure from the settlers to find a way to stop the attacks. Under the unique government arrangements of the day, Governor Evans shared command of all troops then operating in Colorado. The soldiers in the territory were virtually all Colorado men who volunteered for duty in the absence of army regulars, all of whom were off fighting the Civil War. The arrangement allowed either the governor or the US military commander of the Division of the Missouri, Major Samuel Curtis, to control the soldiers in Colorado.

Evans pressured the beleaguered Colonel Chivington—who was now under army orders to control the vast prairie from the Rocky Mountains to the Kansas border (an area of roughly 80,000 square miles) —to find a way to stop the trouble. Chivington could barely keep up with the flood of reports, much less stop the trouble. He rounded up all the soldiers he could find and sent them into the field, ordering those already out to remain in the field until the trouble could be halted.

Chivington again dispatched Lieutenant Eayre and his 100 men who had just returned to Camp Weld (located on the west bank of the Platte River, about two miles northwest of downtown Denver). Their new orders were to locate and pacify the hostile Indians on the plains directly east of Denver. Lieutenant Eayre took with him two of the highly mobile mountain howitzers.

Saturday, May 7. Lieutenant Eayre found a fresh trail made by approximately 100 Indians. He cautioned his men that this was a sizable number, and that if the braves were hostile the soldiers were in for a tough battle. One of Eayre's subordinates, Lieutenant Augustus W. Burton, later told of his instructions from Eayre to "kill Cheyennes whenever and wherever they are found."

Monday, May 16. Lieutenant Eayre's troops were still following the Indian trail eastward, and had reached the Smoky Hill River basin of western Kansas. As the soldiers topped a ridge shortly after lunch, they were attacked by a huge group of Indian soldiers. Army reports later estimated 400 braves may have been in the attacking party. Quickly dismounting, the soldiers fought back in a vicious battle that raged for more than seven hours. When darkness at last fell, the Indians withdrew.

As was often the case with clashes such as these, it was difficult to get an accurate report on casualties on either side. Indians carried away their casualties and didn't keep written records. Army reports were probably only marginally accurate in terms of estimating Indian casualties, although one assumes the military records were accurate in terms of soldiers killed and wounded. The official report filed by Lieutenant Eayre says that twenty-five to thirty Indians were killed, including three Cheyenne chiefs. The report does not further identify the chiefs, nor mention the number of Indians wounded.

Two years later, Indians told white traders that the village near the battleground contained only peaceful Indians, who were innocent of any wrong doing. They said they were camping quietly, and the soldiers attacked without warning. According to the Cheyennes, Chiefs Lean Bear, Black Kettle, and Wolf Chief were in the village at the time of the white man's assault. When they saw the soldiers approaching, Chief Lean Bear walked out to greet the troops and to show them a medal he received while visiting Washington, DC., in 1862. The Indians said that a soldier shot the chief without warning, opening the battle.

As the long battle progressed (according to the Indians' account), the soldiers were driven back and in severe danger of being overrun. However, Chief Black Kettle suddenly appeared, riding calmly among the braves and urging them to stop fighting and to pull back. They maintained that only the intervention of Black Kettle prevented the Indians from wiping out Eayre's entire command.

Some time later, when the US Congress investigated this incident, George Bent (the former Confederate soldier and one of the leaders of the Dog Soldiers) testified that the white soldiers started the battle. Bent maintained that the soldiers were "known to be under orders from Colonel Chivington to kill all the Indians they came across." Bent said the soldiers were saved from destruction when Chief Black Kettle ordered his warriors to pull back.[11]

Author Paul Wellman is among many students of the old West who believe that whites were unnecessarily hostile and aggressive in eastern Colorado, and that the soldiers may have triggered this battle and others. Wellman wrote that Lieutenant Eayre's troops attacked the Indians, and that the attack was "unprovoked and unnecessary." In discussing white–Indian relations in general, Wellman said:

> There was the unprovoked attack by Lieutenant George Eayre and his men on a Cheyenne village...in which a score of Indians were killed. And there were plenty of other crimes of similar nature to be laid at the white man's door.[12]

Regardless of whether the army's version or the Indians' version of the battle is correct, it appears that the positions of both whites and Native Americans hardened significantly in the wake of Eayre's battle with the Cheyennes. Several reports said Southern Cheyennes who had not earlier done so, now smoked the war pipe and agreed to join the northern Cheyennes, the Sioux, and other tribes in an all-out war against whites.

An internal army memo at the time warned that the battle between Eayre and the Cheyennes made it clear that no one was safe now from Indian attack, "even a heavily armed troop of 100 men."

Monday, May 16. Troops under Major Downing encountered several braves east of Greeley, driving a number of horses and mules. When the Indians spotted the soldiers approaching, they abandoned the animals and fled; Downing gave chase, but the braves escaped after a brief running gun battle, with no casualties reported. Downing recovered four mules abandoned by the Indians; all four bore the US Army brand. The Indians would later claim they had found the mules wandering on the prairie and were taking them to an army fort to turn them back over their owners. They said they fled when the troops approached because they feared the soldiers would attack them.

Tuesday, May 17. A white settler rode into Salina, Kansas, and reported that Indians were attacking ranches all along a road running between Fort Riley, Kansas, and Fort Larned, Colorado. The Indian wife of a white settler said that Indians had raided her ranch on Walnut Creek, but spared her and her family because of her Indian blood. The attackers told her they were on the war path and intended to kill all the whites they could find.

H.L. Jones, the deputy United States Marshal at Salina, Kansas, telegraphed the information to Fort Riley. Then Jones rounded up all the men he could find—twelve civilians and about fifteen soldiers who chanced to be in town at the time—and rode out to check ranches on Walnut Creek. At Cow Creek Station, a stop for the Overland Stage Coach Company, Jones found the station master tied to a fence "with an arrow protruding from his forehead." The posse found no other victims, but did locate a number of ranches that had recently been deserted, looted, and burned.[13]

Monday, May 23. An unconfirmed report reached Governor Evans that a large company of soldiers, possibly Lieutenant Eayre's command, was attacked and wiped out in a battle on the Colorado–Kansas border. This report proved to be inaccurate. Another report reached Evans saying that a scouting party of ten soldiers had been butchered on Box Elder Creek in eastern Colorado. A third report said 160 Cheyenne warriors were heading toward the South Platte (from the Arkansas River valley of southeastern Colorado), intent on killing all the white men they could find. Colonel Chivington told Governor Evans there was no immediate way to determine whether any of the reports were true.

Whether or not the reports were true, Evans was understandably alarmed. He telegraphed the United States War Department, the Bureau of Indian Affairs, and General Samuel Curtis, demanding that federal troops be sent to defend Colorado from what he called "this powerful combination of Indian tribes who are pledged to drive all whites from the Territory."[14]

General Curtis responded to Evans by ordering Brigadier General Robert B. Mitchell to defend the North and South Platte River valleys, and Colorado's Colonel Chivington to defend the Arkansas valley. Curtis warned Chivington that Confederate agents were stirring up Indians in the area, and that the Confederates might be planning a direct invasion of Kansas and Colorado.[15]

On that same day, several traders reported to Fort Lyon (in eastern Colorado) that Cheyennes, Kiowas, and Comanches in southern Colorado were now officially on the war path against whites. Colonel Chivington reacted by ordering all available men from the First and Second Colorado Volunteers into the Arkansas Valley. He telegraphed a message to Major Wynkoop at Fort Lyon, saying that things were so bad that only a sound whipping would stop the Indian rebellion.

Saturday, May 28. Governor Evans telegraphed General Curtis at Fort Leavenworth, Kansas, saying that Indians now controlled virtually all of the Great Plains east of Denver. With all major transportation routes to Denver cut off, a full-scale war would soon erupt unless the army did something quickly.

Monday, June 6. A sizable war party attacked a supply train on Coal Creek road just west of Denver. Two men from the supply train were wounded in the attack, and the raiders took all the horses and supplies from the wagon train. Almost simultaneously, another group of warriors attacked a wagon train about sixty-five miles east of Denver at Bijou Creek, taking all the horses and mules. Three men were killed and scalped in the attack, although five others managed to escape.

Saturday, June 11. Upon arriving at Fort Lyon, John Chivington sent a telegram to General Curtis saying, "All signs indicate the Cheyennes and Kiowas are determined to wage war against whites." However, Chivington found no evidence of Comanche or Kiowa-Apache involvement in the hostilities. Chivington related his belief that he now had ample strength to defeat hostile Indians or drive them from the territory, if that was what General Curtis wanted. In order to stop the Confederate influence among Indians, Chivington suggested, "[I] am prepared to move south and attack Confederates in Oklahoma or Texas, if so ordered."

Notes

1. Paul I. Wellman, *Death On The Prairie* (University of Nebraska Press, Lincoln/London, 1934), 374.
2. David Berthrong, *The Southern Cheyennes* (University of Oklahoma Press, 1975), 174.
3. Ibid., 175.
4. Official Records, United States Department of War, 1864, vol. 2,336.
5. Ibid., 176–7.
6. Josephy says that when Colonel Collins first assumed command at Fort Laramie, there were rumors that Indians in the area were being agitated by Confederate agents; most soldiers and settlers believed that's why local Indians had become so hostile. The suspicion was never proved one way or the other. Alvin Josephy, *The Civil War in the American West*, (Alfred A. Knopf, New York, 1991), 247.

7. *The Southern Cheyennes*, 177.
8. Official Records, vol. 2, 337.
9. Duane Shultz, *The Month of the Freezing Moon*, (St. Martin's Press, New York, 1990), claims that the captured Indian was tortured by Major Downing. Shultz does not document the report that says the brave's legs were held over a camp fire until he agreed to lead the troops to the Indian camp. That charge apparently was not officially made at the time, and army records indicate only that the brave was threatened with being shot. There are other references in history, however, which indicate that this sort of fire torture was sometimes used by field commanders to force captive Indians to give information. However, it may also be worth noting that elsewhere in *The Month Of The Freezing Moon* there is misinformation on many other items, including an accusation that John Chivington printed counterfeit US Treasury notes two years earlier. The notes were actually printed on the instructions of Governor William Gilpin, and there is no evidence of Chivington's connection to the incident.
10. *Death On The Prairie*, 87–8.
11. No evidence was ever presented indicating that Bent was at this battle, nor that he had any personal knowledge of the incidents to which he testified.
12. David Lavender, *Bent's Fort* (University of Nebraska Press, Lincoln/London, 1954), 377.
13. *The Southern Cheyennes*, 184.
14. *Civil War in the American West*, 300.
15. The current Confederate pledge to the Indians was that if they helped defeat whites in Colorado, the South would give all of the Great Plains back to the Indians except for a "small, safe corridor" running from west Texas to California.

–FIVE–

The Pace Quickens

FROM THROUGHOUT EASTERN COLORADO and western Kansas the reports began to mount with alarming regularity; ranches burned, cattle stolen, wagon trains looted, whites tortured and murdered. Colonel Chivington was hard-pressed to simply keep up with the reports, much less find the manpower to do something about the trouble. It was as if the raiders knew that most soldiers had left the territory and these Great Plains newcomers were virtually helpless.

Chivington scrambled not only for men, but for leaders. Based on Major Downing's recent report praising young Lieutenant Clark Dunn for bravery under fire and leadership skills, Chivington chose Dunn to lead an important search for a particular group of raiders. No one could have known at the time that this expedition would forever become one focal point in the dispute as to whether whites mistreated plains Indians and were unnecessarily aggressive and cruel toward them.

Dunn, forty men, and five Indian scouts were dispatched on April 21 to a point near modern-day Wray,

Colorado, to search for a herd of twenty horses stolen from a rancher named Ivan Rippey. Rippey asked to join the search, and Dunn was quick to accept his company— not only because Rippey could identify any animals recovered, but because his presence gave the searchers one more rifle in the event of trouble.

It was not difficult to follow the trail of the stolen animals; snow was still melting from the prairie and the herd's hoof prints were clearly visible in the mud and snow. The soldiers followed the trail of the missing herd for four days. On the afternoon of April 25, they spotted a sizeable herd of horses and many—perhaps sixty— braves on the west bank of the Platte River near Sterling. Dunn cautioned his men to be prepared for anything, but not to appear aggressive.

The Indians guarding the herd of horses spotted the soldiers at the same time the soldiers spotted them. Turning to face the on-coming troops, the warriors lined up side by side across a shallow valley through which the trail passed. What transpired in the next few minutes will always be a matter of great debate.

The braves would later claim that it was the soldiers who began shooting; as the soldiers drew near, three warriors were suddenly shot from their ponies. They would say they battled back in self defense and the soldiers soon ran for their lives, leaving one dead soldier on the battlefield. The braves said one of the warriors later decapitated the dead soldier and took his uniform, which they subsequently traded to a band of Brule Sioux[1] near Fort Laramie. The Cheyennes then asked the Brules to join them in an all-out attack against all whites in the area.

George Bent, who was becoming more and more militant, would later claim that Lieutenant Dunn's patrol had actually come across a small, peaceful band of Indians who were driving their own horses. Bent admitted that some of Rippey's horses may have been in the Indian herd; but if so, they were strays and, under the white man's laws, could be claimed by whomever captured them. Although there is no evidence that Bent was in northeastern Colorado at the time of the incident or that his facts were accurate, history has recorded his testimony as the absolute truth.[2] The Bent testimony was also later widely quoted in Eastern newspapers to show that it was whites who were the aggressors; the opposing testimony of Lieutenant Dunn and his men would forever be virtually ignored.

Lieutenant Dunn's version of the confrontation and battle gives an entirely different picture. Significantly, Dunn and every man in his command gave the same version of the incident. According to their story, when the warriors were spotted, the soldiers slowed down and approached cautiously, stopping entirely when the two sides were about 500 yards apart. The Indians immediately formed a battle line, weapons ready, as they faced the approaching soldiers.

A small stream separated the two sides. The soldiers began moving forward cautiously, and when the two parties were about 100 yards apart the soldiers had reached the banks of the river. Dunn stopped his patrol and told the men to water their horses. While they did so, Dunn and rancher Rippey went forward a short distance to meet the braves. According to this version, Dunn and Rippey had their weapons holstered to show that they wanted only to talk. Dunn estimated there were sixty warriors in the group he was facing. He and Rippey both testified that Rippey was immediately able to identify many of his missing horses among the animals in the Indian herd.

Dunn noticed that several other braves had begun driving the horse herd on down the trail, while these warriors blocked the road between the soldiers and the animals. Dunn says he turned toward his own lines and ordered his men to cut off the trail, and not permit the herd to be driven any further while he talked with the Indian leader. Since Dunn did not speak their language, he selected a soldier who did so to act as interpreter. The soldier left his rifle in the saddle scabbard, dismounted, and walked alone toward the Indians. He asked the chief to return the stolen horses to the soldiers. Dunn's report says the chief laughed scornfully at this request; at that point, the lieutenant realized that an armed confrontation was inevitable.

Dunn then dismounted, walked forward, and joined his interpreter in talking with the Indian leaders. In writing of the incident later, Dunn said the warriors had their bows strung (in battle readiness) with arrows in place, and had their rifles loaded in a threatening manner. Dunn's soldiers were shouting at him to return to friendly lines, fearing that he would be seized and killed. Dunn ordered the interpreter back to his horse, whereupon both men turned their backs to the foe, and strode back to friendly lines. As they moved, the Indians moved also, riding along at the heels of the two soldiers. Dunn shouted at his men to hold their fire, but that if the warriors continued to approach, to disarm and capture them.

When Dunn reached his ranks, the Indians were only a few feet behind. His troops dismounted, and the enemy suddenly opened fire. The soldiers returned the fire and, in their version of the incident, it was the Indians who turned and fled after a one-hour battle. Four of the soldiers were hit by gunfire, two of whom were fatally wounded.[3]

According to the army report, Lieutenant Dunn and his soldiers pursued the Indians in a running gun battle that covered a distance of about sixteen miles. Eventually, the warriors split into numerous small groups and fled in different directions; the soldiers—exhausted from a long ride and the gun battle—soon abandoned the chase.

Shortly thereafter, a spring snowstorm swept the area. By morning, all signs of the escaping Indians had been obliterated by new-fallen snow. The soldiers gave up on the pursuit and returned to base. Dunn says his soldiers killed eight to ten braves during the hour-long battle and the chase that followed; the soldiers suffered two dead and two wounded in the encounter.

By this time, there were two distinct types of Indians in Colorado. The first group consisted of those who were peaceful and compliant, who were willing to become farmers, live on reservations, and wanted no part of war; for the most part, these were the older members of all tribes. These groups generally lived quietly near settlements or forts; many of them camped permanently near Bent's Fort on the Arkansas River.

The second group of Indians was angry and defiant, determined to drive white men from the region, and willing to do whatever it took (including rape, murder, arson, and thievery) to achieve this goal. They justified these attacks as self-defense: a matter of life and death for the Indian culture. This pro–war group, which included the Dog Soldiers and other soldier societies—consisted primarily of the young warriors, mostly braves who were in their late teens or twenties. They were strong, clever, mobile—and angry.

George and Charles Bent were among the militant younger Indians. Both were regularly reported to be among Indian groups attacking various targets. The

Bent brothers were easy to recognize because of their
mixed ancestry and mostly caucasian features, and the
brothers appeared intent on making their participation
known to any who survived their attacks. In at least one
case, they actually introduced themselves to men whom
they permitted to survive.

As the spring of 1864 developed, scores of militant
Indians were living in small villages scattered across
the eastern Colorado prairie. Ruth Dunn, writer and
historian, says George Bent boasted of these villages'
immunity from white attack. All of the villages were
"filled with plunder from captured or burned wagon
trains. Both [Indian] men and women had the finest silk
cloaks and bonnets."[4]

Author David Lavender wrote that by early
summer of 1864:

> Each [Indian] village echoed to the shrieks of the scalp
> dance. Almost daily war parties arrived with plunder
> from the merchandise trains. Indian braves strutted
> in ladies' bonnets. Colored silks were sewn into garish
> dresses for the squaws and shirts for the young men.
> George [Bent] had a half-dozen made. An estimated
> 200 travelers and settlers were killed; scores of lonely
> ranches burned to the ground. A few women captives
> survived; one of them, Mrs. Eubanks, probably
> testifies for all; "An old chief forced me, by the most
> terrible threats and menaces, to yield my person to
> him." When the chief was through with her, he passed
> her on to others.[5]

In fact, the situation on the plains was so bad that
travel from Denver eastward was becoming impossible.
Wagon trains simply couldn't get through; they were
attacked, looted, burned and their teamsters killed.
Often the captured travelers were horribly tortured.
White women taken prisoner were raped over and over

again by all the men of the war party, then traded to some other tribe where the entire process was repeated.

Freight companies soon quit shipping anything to Denver, and the white settlements of Colorado became completely isolated. They could not get food or supplies from outside sources. Machinery or tools that broke could not be repaired or replaced. The white population, already struggling with food shortages because of the drought, was getting more and more desperate. In some places there were signs of panic, and in all the settlements the Indian was held completely responsible for the problem. Those who had previously taken a moderate stance toward the Indians became hardened against them; the chasm between the two cultures widened significantly.

Governor Evans sent several telegrams to Washington, demanding that something be done to protect the citizens of Colorado. The government, caught up in the Civil War, didn't even bother to respond. The army did a little better; it notified battlefield commanders in the region that they would have to get tougher in dealing with Indians. In western Kansas, Lieutenant George Stilwell was chewed out by his commander for not being tough enough on Indians, so Stilwell instructed his men, "just be sure you have the right ones, then kill 'em."

Colonel Chivington telegraphed Colonel Collins at Fort Laramie to report the incident involving Lieutenant Dunn's command. Chivington presumed that the responsible Indians were heading north, toward Fort Laramie. Under the latest orders from the military command the colonel suggested that "when you find them, kill them!"[6] Chivington also wrote a letter to General Samuel Curtis to report the Dunn incident, saying that if he caught the guilty Indians he planned to punish them severely, "unless you direct otherwise." General Curtis, preoccupied in the desperate defense of Missouri which was under attack by a large Confederate army, did not reply to Chivington's letter. His failure to do so was widely interpreted as a decision to let his previous orders stand: guilty Indians were to be punished severely.

The reports of new Indian raids seemed to increase daily, almost hourly. The few soldiers available were in the field constantly, trying to track down stolen animals or find and free captured white women.

Lieutenant Dunn and Lieutenant George Chase reported trailing one large herd of stolen animals, but another surprise spring snowstorm obliterated the trail northeast of Greeley, and the troops gave up. As the soldiers headed back toward Denver, they chanced across another ranch that had just been raided. Several ranch buildings were still on fire, and the body of the rancher was found near one of the buildings; he had been scalped. Leading away from the ranch, the soldiers found a trail made by about forty steers. Apparently they had been taken from a corral behind the burning barn. The direction of the trail led the army to conclude that the attack was made by southern Cheyennes.

In Denver, the *Rocky Mountain News* ran a front page editorial, demanding Governor Evans and Colonel Chivington do more to protect Colorado from Indian attack. The editorial was particularly stinging, given the fact that editor William Byers was a close personal friend of the two men he chastised in the article. Byers insisted that Evans and Chivington "do the necessary thing" to stop Indian raids.

Retired BIA agent Albert Boone—a defender of Indians (and a nephew of Daniel Boone)—wrote to Chivington, demanding more military protection for his farm near La Junta. Even those Indians Boone previously considered to be friendly were now openly hostile. In response to the agent's letter, Chivington sent two regiments from the old First and Second Colorado Volunteers to reinforce Camp Fillmore and several other small military outposts scattered along the Arkansas River.

At Fort Lyon, several friendly Indians reported that numerous stolen horses and steers were among a large Cheyenne herd being kept on Sand Creek, not far from the fort. Captain David L. Hardy and fifty soldiers were sent out from the fort to find and recover the animals, even if it meant an armed confrontation with the Indians.

Indian Agent Colley was at Fort Lyon when the troops rode out. Colley (who was usually considered to be a friend of all Indians) warned Captain Hardy that most southern Cheyennes had not accepted any war pipe and were not hostile. But Colley admitted that it was impossible to tell which Cheyennes were friendly and which considered themselves to be at war with the whites. His statements pinpointed one of the army's most serious problems: there was no way to distinguish friendly Indians from those who had deadly intentions.

Within hours, Captain Hardy located a large herd of animals guarded by several Cheyenne warriors. When he was able to identify a number of the animals as having been stolen from several nearby ranches, the Indians readily surrendered the stock. The braves said the animals were strays that had simply wandered into their camp.

In his report on the incident, Captain Hardy said the Indians seemed genuine; their story about strays was probably true. The Cheyenne braves expressed great fear that they would linked to the violent raids now occurring throughout Colorado. They blamed the latest raids on northern Cheyennes and Sioux,[7] and some sources suggested that Confederate agitators most likely were stirring up, arming, and training the militants.

As if all of this pressure was not enough, another disaster hit Denver. On Thursday, May 19, 1864, a cloudburst sent a wall of water rushing down Cherry Creek through the heart of the city. Scores of buildings were destroyed, including the offices and presses of the *Rocky Mountain News*. Ten persons were killed, and the flood destroyed several warehouses of food—making the food shortage even more pressing than before.

Saturday, June 11. Prominent rancher Isaac P. Van Wormer left his ranch at Elizabeth, southeast of Denver, and went into town to buy supplies. Two of Van Wormer's hired hands, foreman Ward Hungate and cowboy Edgar Miller, remained at the ranch, repairing fences.

The two men were over a mile from the ranch buildings when they spotted clouds of thick black smoke, rising into the air from the general direction of the ranch house. Miller leaped on his horse and rode toward a neighboring ranch to summon help. Hungate raced back toward the ranch house, where his wife and two little girls were staying.

Miller reached the next ranch and sounded the alarm. The neighbor quickly rounded up a half-dozen cowboys, and raced toward the Van Wormer ranch. When they arrived, they found all the buildings burned to the ground. Fences were cut, and all the horses and cattle were missing.

The body of Ward Hungate was found lying in the main road, numerous arrows protruding from his head and body. After searching for some time they found the bodies of his wife and two little girls, one and four years old,[8] bound and thrown into a well. Mrs. Hungate's body was nude; she had been repeatedly raped. Other evidence suggested that she and the little girls had been brutally tortured before their deaths. Mrs. Hungate had been burned and slashed with a knife. The throats of the little girls had been cut, their heads nearly severed from their bodies. Their abdomens were ripped open and their entrails dragged out. All three had been scalped.

The bodies of the four Hungates were loaded onto a flatbed wagon and hauled into Denver. Several hundred people crowded around the wagon to view the grisly sight. Before long, a large angry mob had formed and marched over to the state house (the building housing the offices of the territorial governor and other appointed officials) to demand revenge.

At about the same time, some of the men who had found the bodies rode into Denver. They reported that while scouring the countryside around the Van Wormer ranch, they talked to other ranchers who said a sizable number of Cheyenne Dog Soldiers were riding through the area that day. Several ranchers claimed that the notorious and militant chief Roman Nose (who, because of his enormous size, was fairly easy to identify) was leading the Dog Soldiers.[9]

Governor Evans summoned Colonel Chivington to his office while the mob was still present, and demanded to know how such an atrocity could have been carried out—especially so close to Denver. Colonel Chivington's response to Governor Evans is not recorded, but his actions are. He ordered Lieutenant Clark Dunn to "track down the Indians who did this," and that if Dunn found the guilty Indians he was not to encumber himself with prisoners.[10]

There immediately arose a debate as to the identity of the Indians involved in the Hungate killings. There was strong circumstantial evidence linking Roman Nose and Cheyenne Dog Soldiers to the atrocity, including those eyewitness reports that placed Roman Nose in the area, but there is at least some credible evidence that the murders may have been the work of four Arapaho warriors.

A fur trader named Robert North claimed that a fellow fur trapper, John Notee, had been caught red-handed with stolen horses belonging to Van Wormer. North claimed that when the soldiers took back the horses, Notee was furious and vowed to get revenge against Van Wormer. Notee was later questioned by soldiers about the Hungate killings, but emphatically denied involvement or knowledge of the killings. He said the word among Indians was that Roman Nose and the Dog Soldiers had committed the crime.

Regardless of who was guilty, it was obvious that the Hungate murders were committed by a number of Indians, and the brutality of the killings whipped emotions to a fury. The citizens of Colorado were unified in demanding swift and decisive military action against all hostile Indians in the territory.

The mood of the citizenry, combined with the lack of food and supplies in Denver, prompted Governor Evans to wire another telegram to the area's US Army commander, General Samuel Curtis:

> It will be the destruction and death to Colorado if our lines of communication are cut off or if they are not kept so securely guarded as that freighters will not be afraid to cross the plains. We are now short of provisions and but few trains are on the way. I respectfully ask that our troops (the Third Colorado Volunteers) be allowed to defend us.[11]

General Curtis wired back to Governor Evans a formal authorization to activate the Third Colorado. He also authorized Colonel Chivington to take the troops into the field "to crush the Indians that are in open hostilities."[12]

Notes

1. There were five major divisions of the Sioux tribe; the Brules were considered the most aggressive and the least friendly to whites.

2. In statements given to congressional investigators more than a year after this incident, both George Bent and frontiersman Kit Carson would claim that the army horses in the Indian herd had probably simply wandered away from lazy herders, who then blamed the Indians for the disappearance. The book by David Berthrong, *The Southern Cheyennes* (University of Oklahoma Press, 1975), 178–80, quotes Bent as if his testimony was completely and unquestionably true; author Berthrong says "both Crow Chief's band and Beaver's village [the two Indian groups whose men participated in the skirmish with Dunn] were totally innocent of the theft and unaware of any difficulty with whites."

3. Excerpted from the transcript of the Chivington investigation by the US Army as quoted in the book by John Chivington, *To the People of Colorado: Synopsis of the Sand Creek Investigation* (Wagner-Camp, Denver, June, 1865).

4. Ruth Dunn, "Attack on Black Kettle's Village," unpublished notes, Heritage Collection, Lincoln, Nebraska Public Library, 8.

5. David Lavender, *Bent's Fort* (University of Nebraska Press, Lincoln/London, 1954), 380.

6. Ibid., 380.

7. David Berthrong, *The Southern Cheyennes* (University of Oklahoma Press, 1975), 180.

8. Some accounts of history list the girls' ages as seven and four.

9. *The Southern Cheyennes,* 184. However, it should be noted that in spite of his enormous stature and recognizable features, other Indians were often mis-identified as being Roman

Nose; the "positive identification" of him in this case was speculative at best.

10. Ibid., 190. Although most accounts of this tragedy add the line about Chivington telling his men not to "encumber themselves with prisoners," we can find no place that quote is attributed to any source or record. Whether Chivington actually issued such an order is debatable.

11. Ibid., 191.

12. Ibid., 191.

–SIX–

Unlimited War

THE GRUESOME MUTILATION MURDERS of the Hungate family revolted and outraged people all over the West, but especially those in Colorado. The rape-murders served as a catalyst for hatred and seemed to mark the beginning of an all-out, undeclared war against Indians. It was as if they were suddenly "in season" and could be—perhaps should be—attacked whenever and wherever they were located.

There was a run on guns and ammunition at local stores throughout the frontier. Little groups of men stood around Denver and other communities talking about forming their own army and going after the Indians, since the government seemed unwilling or unable to deal with the problem. Governor Evans recognized the signs of panic, and recognized that the civilians in the territory were on the verge of becoming an uncontrollable mob; he repeatedly appealed for calm.

In public statements made at several locations, Governor Evans argued that a citizen's army, improperly armed and inadequately trained, would not know where to look for hostile groups. He feared that the deployment of such troops would result in the death or injury of innocent people on both sides. Evans reminded citizens that it would be un–Christian behavior, and a terrible mistake, to attack friendly Indians. Realizing something must be done, Evans promised to take swift, decisive action to find and punish those who killed the Hungate family.

In spite of the general mood, Governor Evans kept cautioning against haste or mistaken attacks against friendly Indians. Twenty-five years earlier, a civilian posse attacked peaceful Indians in Texas, triggering a bloody all-out war. The resulting war cost hundreds of lives. Evans may have had such incidents in mind when he suggested the first thing that ought to be done was to establish special "peace camps" for any tribal groups who did not want to wage war. Such camps would receive those who were friendly, and keep them out of harms way during the army's show-down fight with unfriendly groups. Evans' warning was clear: failure to report to one of the peace camps would subject them to possible attack.

Saturday, June 18, 1864. Governor Evans wrote a letter to the Bureau of Indian affairs, announcing that he had ordered the establishment of peace camps. Friendly tribal groups throughout the plains were instructed to report to certain locations (such as Bent's Fort and Fort Lyon); any who failed to report would be considered enemies, and would be attacked. Evans expressed his hope that friendly bands would respond to this order. Then, as the hostile Indians were whipped, all the Plains tribes would either be driven to their knees in surrender, or agree to peaceful co-existence with whites; finally bringing peace to Colorado and the West.

Courtesy Colorado Historical Society

JOHN EVANS, GOVERNOR OF COLORADO

Evans appealed repeatedly to the national government for help in dealing with the "Indian problem," and warned that without federal help the growing dispute would result in a bloody, all-out war. Washington ignored him.

Evans said he had established camps in enough locations, including one at Fort Larned and another on the Cache La Poudre River near Fort Collins, so that there would be a camp at a convenient site no matter where the Indian people were. Evans suggested that making it easy for them was important: history had shown that failure to correctly locate a meeting place resulted in failure.

His last sentence was apparently a dig at the BIA. Several years earlier the agency had tried to get Native groups to attend peace talks; but the tribes in southeastern Colorado and Kansas were to report to Fort Laramie, and those in Wyoming and Nebraska were to attend meetings in far southern Colorado. The talks resulted in complete failure.

Evans had never enjoyed a close relationship with the BIA. He considered it to be a bungling, bureaucratic, inefficient, and ineffective federal agency that meddled in frontier affairs. As most other westerners, Evans believed the BIA did not understand what was really happening in the West—or didn't care. His attitude may have been responsible, in part, to the BIA's response to his plan—and to the tragedies that followed.

The Commissioner of Indian Affairs at that time was Charles E. Mix, described as a "high handed Minnesotan with a record of...defrauding Indians"[1] and as a man who, along with other government officials was "habitually elbow-deep in fraud."[2] Mix appeared both surprised and offended that Governor Evans had "interfered" in Indian matters, an arena Mix considered to be his private domain. Mix stunned the West by flatly rejecting Evans' plan, even though it had already been announced and was in the process of being implemented.

Commissioner Mix wrote a strongly worded letter back to Governor Evans, saying that because of the continuing Civil War there simply was no money to set up his proposed Colorado camps, nor to feed and care for any who surrendered at such camps. Apparently referring to the unauthorized expenditures by Evans' predecessor, Governor John Gilpin (who issued phony US Treasury notes to pay for the First and Second Colorado Volunteers), Mix cautioned Evans to "make certain you contract no debt for the feeding of Indians."[3]

There is considerable doubt whether Evans had any legal right to order establishment of the "friendly Indian" camps, but there is even greater doubt whether the BIA had any right to tell the governor of a territory what to do or not to do. After the exchange of unfriendly missives, however, Mix clearly presumed that Evans would not establish the peace camps, nor would he try to get any peaceful groups to surrender at any forts or camps in Colorado.

The BIA's rejection of Governor Evans' plan left Colorado in a deep dilemma. Citizens of the territory were demanding swift and decisive action, and were on the verge of taking matters into their own hands. The army had already endorsed a "no-holds barred" policy toward Indians, saying that any hostile groups should be "wiped out." The Department of War had tacitly approved the policy that called for extermination of hostile factions, but warned that it could send no more troops to help carry out such an eradication. At this point, the BIA didn't care what Colorado did so long as Evans didn't set up peace camps or spend any money to take care of those who wanted to stay out of the battle. Add to that volatile mixture the fact that friendly Indian people were already beginning to show up at Evan's announced peace camps, expecting to be fed and protected during the upcoming war.

Faced with those seemingly irreconcilable differences, and knowing that he had to do something before armed civilians went out looking for hostile factions, Evans decided to institute a modified version of his peace camps, in spite of BIA opposition. Risking increased hostility from the Bureau, Evans sent messengers to notify all tribes in Colorado that tribal groups must move quickly to military outposts in Colorado and surrender "so that we will know you are not hostile." He warned that any who failed to set up camp at an army outpost would be considered hostile, subject to being shot on site.

The citizens of Colorado—and their newspapers—cheered the governor's hard-nosed approach to the problem and his order to the Indian people to either give up or be attacked. They believed Evans had clearly and fairly paved the way for identifying and then wiping out those hostile parties who had killed the Hungates and—for whatever reasons—had committed hundreds of other atrocities against whites.

In the midst of celebrating the governor's action, no one apparently stopped to consider whether the instructions were clear enough to eliminate any possibility of misunderstanding. As it turned out, confusion over the instructions did arise, and may have contributed to the tragedy that soon followed—and to a controversy that still rages 125 years later.

One of the key areas of uncertainty was the question of what constituted a friendly Indian camp "at" the various forts in Colorado. With the exact boundaries beyond which they would not be "at" a fort undefined, the definition was left to the individuals—and that would prove to be a grievous error.

Hundreds responded to Evans' warning and began camping around various forts in Colorado. At each newly established camp, the people were questioned about the Hungate murders.

Courtesy Colorado Historical Society

ROMAN NOSE, DOG SOLDIER CHIEF

One of the renegade young warriors, Roman Nose may have been the greatest Indian"general" of all time. Roman Nose was impervious to the white man's bullets, and threatened to kill any Indian who refused to join him in attacking white soldiers.

Many, including several hundred southern Cheyenne and Arapaho warriors who surrendered at Fort Lyon, unhesitatingly blamed the murders on Cheyenne war chief Roman Nose and his Dog Soldiers. Arapaho chief Neva said unequivocally that Roman Nose was personally involved in the killings, and that Roman Nose and three of his warriors had raped and tortured Mrs. Hungate and murdered the children. Since the reports blaming Roman Nose came from a dozen different locations and all contained roughly the same information, virtually all concerned believed this information to be accurate.

But even as many tribal groups were surrendering, many others were not.

Thursday, June 23. A family of five was killed and scalped, and their ranch burned near Greeley. Approximately a half dozen horses were taken by the attackers.

Several hours after the Greeley attack, a family of three was found dead beside their burned-out wagon a few miles east of Loveland. They, too, had been scalped.

Friday, June 24. A married couple and two ranch hands were killed in an attack near Pueblo. The ranch buildings were set afire and several horses run off.

Clearly, an all-out war was being waged by some tribal factions; nearly everyone assumed that those responsible were Cheyenne, and especially Cheyenne Dog Soldiers.

Saturday, June 25. An army patrol found six buffalo hunters killed and scalped near Cheyenne Wells. Their camp had been ransacked and their horses were missing. Arrows at the scene suggested the attackers were probably Cheyennes.

That morning, Governor Evans issued a strongly worded proclamation to the citizens of Colorado. In part, the governor said:

> As these murderous [Indian] raids continue, it becomes increasingly clear that we cannot count on help from the United States government. We are on our own to defend our families and our property. It is of no use to negotiate further with these hostile Indians. They have shown that discussion and negotiation are meaningless to them. Therefore, I hereby call on all citizens of Colorado Territory to kill and otherwise destroy all such hostile Indians, and hold all property of said hostile Indians.[4]

Sunday, July 3. A report reached Governor Evans concerning evidence in the Hungate murders, quoting statements by Arapaho chief Neva. The chief blamed Roman Nose for the slaughter. So did several army officers—based on testimonies of various peaceful Indians who had stated they "knew for a fact" that Roman Nose was to blame for the Hungate murders and for others.

On that afternoon, Evans received another troubling report from two fur traders. Robert North and William McGaa told the governor that angry Cheyennes were trying to get all other tribes in the area to join them in an all-out war against whites. But the reports had an ominous new twist: they said that Dog Soldiers were now threatening to kill any Indians who went to the white man's forts to express their intention of not joining such hostilities.

North and McGaa said Roman Nose had sent word to all Cheyenne camps that he would personally punish those who refused to fight. If they were outnumbered or unable to attack, Roman Nose instructed them to feign friendship until they were in a position to effectively attack the enemy. Both fur traders said the warring parties claimed to have been hoarding ammunition for eight years in preparation for this total effort to drive whites from their land. If the report was true, the war against white settlers was first suggested and planned as early as 1856.

In light of this troubling new information, Governor Evans telegraphed Secretary of War, Edwin Stanton, asking military funding for the plan to raise the Third Colorado Volunteers. This group would be "100-day soldiers," sworn in merely to protect the citizenry until either the hostilities ended, regular soldiers could return to Colorado, or cold weather cooled emotions both figuratively and literally. Secretary Stanton granted the funding a few days later.

Monday, July 4. A small wagon train was destroyed on the Oregon Trail near Julesburg, Colorado. Four people were killed and scalped, and about forty horses were taken in the attack.

Tuesday, July 5. Governor Evans proclaimed martial law in Colorado, pending resolution of the "Indian trouble." The proclamation temporarily suspended constitutional rights—especially those pertaining to arrest, detainment, and trial.

Thursday, July 7. The War Department formally notified Governor Evans that all available "extra" troops were being ordered back to the Great Plains in an effort to control hostilities and protect settlers, in light of the sharply increased Indian attacks. General Samuel

Curtis was ordered to take all appropriate measures to insure the safety of Kansas and Colorado residents. Curtis, in turn, ordered troops to begin escorting all wagon trains, mail wagons, stage coaches, and individuals traveling on the Oregon, Santa Fe, and Smoky Hill Trails.

Curtis recognized that the frontier was a powder keg, threatening to explode into a war that could rival the Civil War for bloodshed and carnage. The general specifically warned his troops not to be trigger-happy because "it would require but a few murders on our part to unite all the plains Indians in a war [against white settlers]."⁵

Friday, July 8. A war party attacked a stage relay station forty miles east of Denver. The buildings were burned, and thirty-five horses and mules were taken by the raiders. Several people at the station barricaded themselves in an adobe shed and survived the attack.

Saturday, July 9. Governor Evans wrote a lengthy letter to General Curtis, suggesting that the regular army and the not-yet field-ready Third Colorado should coordinate their campaigns to achieve maximum effectiveness. Evans asked Curtis to personally assume responsibility for coordinating plans to stage simultaneous attacks against hostile factions throughout the region.

Evans suggested some specific plans: Colonel Chivington and the new Third Colorado could attack in the south; General Robert Mitchell, out of Fort Laramie, could attack from the north; General Curtis could attack from the east. The only reason to delay or cancel such plans, said Evans, was if General Curtis possessed information (not available elsewhere) that "all the evidence of an Indian war already in progress" was not true.[6]

The governor's letter recounted, in grisly detail, the scores of reports he had received that such a war was already underway. He listed more than fifty individual attacks since the first of the year; Evans did not see how any reasonable man could deny that the Indians had declared war. The governor made it clear that he was pushing for immediate and decisive military action, which he perceived was necessary to save white civilization. It would also, of course, take the heat off the governor's office.

Even as the letter was on its way to General Curtis, several new attacks were reported:

Monday, July 11. A stagecoach traveling between Fort Larned and Fort Lyon was besieged, but a strong military escort drove off the attackers, killing several of them. The coach reached Fort Lyon safely.

Tuesday, July 12. Approximately 150 warriors attacked a four-wagon train traveling from Julesburg, Colorado to Fort Laramie, Wyoming, on the Oregon Trail. The teamsters jumped from the wagons and fled on foot, while their attackers concentrated on capturing the horses and ransacking the wagons. The teamsters identified the enemy as Cheyenne Dog Soldiers.

Wednesday, July 13. Governor Evans ordered all saloons in Colorado be closed "for the duration"—an effort, he said, to make certain that all the citizens of the territory—"white men or their enemies"—would at the very least be sober. Most other businesses closed, as well. Grocery stores in Colorado remained open, but between the drought and the fact that no supplies were coming in from the East, groceries were in such short order that none operated more than a few hours a day anyway.

Friday, July 15. Colonel Chivington received a letter from General Curtis, instructing him to "attend to the Indians" if they were hostile. Curtis's letter commented that a "few well-placed howitzer rounds" ought to take care of most of them. The order seemed logical at the time, but it was one of several that would become the subject of heated debate a few months later.

Sunday, July 17. Large bands of Indians attacked the Bijou, Kelly, and Beaver Creek Overland stage coach relay stations in northeastern Colorado. A military escort commander, Captain George Sanborn, reported five soldiers killed and another wounded in successfully driving off the attackers at Bijou Station. He reported approximately 200 horses stolen from the three stage stops, although most of the horses were found freely roaming the range a short time later, and recaptured.

Sunday afternoon, 2:00 PM. Brigadier General Robert Mitchell telegraphed General Curtis from Fort Laramie. He asked for permission to raise a company of 200 volunteers, from among the ranchers of Wyoming, to defend themselves from increasingly frequent attacks. Mitchell expressed concern that the few soldiers available to him were not capable of dealing with any major attack, nor were they numerous enough to take offensive action against the Indians.

General Curtis, who was not fond of temporary volunteer military units, denied Mitchell's request. However, he noted that Colorado had well organized and well-trained volunteers, apparently referring to the

First and Second Colorado Volunteers. Some of those units, activated into the US Army two years earlier, remained active. Curtis urged Mitchell to take advantage of the availability of these men.

Yet, in spite of all the saber-rattling, the military actually took little action—and the Indian attacks were continuing.

Monday, July 18. A stage coach was attacked and burned near Limon. The five occupants were killed and scalped.

Tuesday, July 19. A small wagon train was wiped out on the Santa Fe Trail, in the southeastern corner of Colorado. Two of the travelers were killed.

Wednesday, July 20. Three buffalo hunters were killed, and two wounded, in a three-hour battle with attacking Indians near the Colorado–Kansas border. That afternoon, two abandoned ranches were burned about thirty miles southeast of Denver. Army patrols reported the fires as deliberately started by "sizable" groups of Indians.

Two more ranches were burned near Limon, seventy miles east of Denver, with six people killed and perhaps 100 horses stolen. A stagecoach was robbed in the vicinity two days earlier.

Thursday, July 21. A mail wagon was burned, and the driver killed and scalped, near Camp Collins, sixty miles north of Denver.

It was clear to citizens of the area (especially those in Denver) that the hostile bands of Indians were attacking when and where they pleased, and the army was incapable of coping with the problem. The *Rocky*

Mountain News carried strongly worded editorials about the federal government's inability or refusal to bring an end to the problem through concentrated military action. The writer recognized that the Civil War was continuing, but said the Union was strong enough now to spare the troops necessary to put down this separate Indian war.

One of the greater problems facing General Curtis, Governor Evans, and other officials was the difficulty in obtaining and exchanging information. It was no longer safe for mail wagons (or other travelers) to try to cross the prairie; on July 22, US Mail service was suspended for an indefinite period of time. To make matters worse, Indian raiders had cut or pulled down most of the telegraph wires across the territory.

About the only way to send information was by personal messenger, and only a large military escort could ensure the messenger's safety. Such correspondence proved to be agonizingly slow. Often, adequate numbers of troops simply were not available for escort duty. As a result, various authorities went for days without being able to communicate with one another. The isolated towns and military posts in Colorado and Kansas were virtually on their own. Of course, the army already knew that its general order was to pursue and stop hostile Indians. Even so, the communication breakdown meant that every individual command had to act independently from its head-quarters.

The day that General Curtis left Fort Leavenworth to personally assume command of the anti–Indian fighting, warriors made a frontal assault against Fort Larned, Colorado. Approximately 300 braves stormed the fort, but for the first time in many months the stockade was heavily defended. The soldiers fired cannons to break up the Indian charge, and inflicted heavy casualties among the attackers; the remaining warriors fled after a brief battle.

Driven from the fort by the unexpectedly strong resistance, the raiders apparently rode directly to the nearby Cow Creek stagecoach relay station. There they attacked and burned the buildings, and killed ten men who had sought shelter at the station. Another man and a boy at the station escaped being killed by pretending to be dead; both were scalped, but survived. Later, both identified their attackers as Cheyenne Dog Soldiers.

Twenty-four hours later, a group from the same war party attacked four small wagon trains traveling along the Smoky Hill Trail, in eastern Colorado. Somehow, the travelers failed to get word of the official road closures in Colorado and western Kansas. In these attacks, thirteen men were killed and approximately 300 horses and mules were driven off.

Altogether, during the 120 hours from July 17 through 21, raids in eastern Colorado resulted in the deaths of about thirty-five men, left three others wounded, forty wagons and nine ranches burned, and 600 horses and mules stolen.

Traders, who continued operating on the plains, reported that Dog Soldiers brought virtually all of the plunder from these raids into their villages. These Cheyennes, camped along the Solomon River in western Kansas, were holding nightly "scalp dances" to celebrate their victories and to display the grisly trophies of their attacks.

The trustworthy William Bent confirmed these reports. He also told BIA agent Colley that the attacks were primarily the work of only about 150 Dog Soldiers, who were no longer taking orders from any of their chiefs. (His estimate either fell far short of reality or army reports were greatly exaggerated—or both. It was common to hear of raiding parties numbering 200 to 400 warriors.)

Monday, July 25. Arriving at Fort Larned, General Curtis received a briefing on a series of battles occurring in the immediate area over the past several days. Being out of touch with other forts because of communication problems, he was uncertain whether similar attacks taking place elsewhere, but must have presumed they were.

Nonetheless, Curtis came to what many consider an incredible conclusion; although there were unquestionably numerous hostile bands operating in eastern Colorado, there was inconclusive evidence of an actual declaration of war by the Indians.

Even with that pronouncement, General Curtis did order the 400 available troops at Fort Larned to spread out along the Santa Fe Trail, in order to stop attacks there. One day later, 150 Indians attacked and wiped out a five-wagon train at Cimmaron Crossing. Two men were killed and scalped, the wagons burned, and forty horses and mules were taken.

BIA agent was thoroughly disgusted with the Indians he had so often defended. He wrote a letter to Governor Evans saying that the Cheyennes were completely out of control, and "a little powder and lead is the best food for them."[7]

General Curtis dispatched a runner to try to locate Colonel Chivington, who was in the field with his troops. The runner returned several days later with information that Chivington had gone back to Denver, either to train troops of the Third Colorado or to hold conferences with Governor Evans.

General Curtis was furious. He believed Chivington had no excuse to leave the battlefield at a time like this. When Curtis eventually made contact with Chivington a few days later, he accused the colonel of having made the trip to Denver solely because of politics—Chivington now being the darling of the Republic party and the likely GOP candidate for Congress.

Chivington was indignant at the accusation. He pointed out that communication with the general (or anyone else) had been impossible for several weeks. During that time, it was necessary for Chivington to act independently of his superiors. Since the only way to make certain a message got delivered was to deliver it in person, he made the trip to Denver. It was vital, he said, that he and Governor Evans exchange information and coordinate plans.

Chivington reminded General Curtis of his specific authorization to activate the Third Colorado Volunteers. These men would be under Chivington's command, and only the Colonel, himself, was in a position to recruit, organize, and train the unit. Those responsibilities required his presence in Denver.

Chivington emphasized the importance of employing these new Colorado recruits on the prairie to relieve army regulars, still needed elsewhere to fight the Civil War. Under existing laws, the Third was jointly under the command of General Curtis and Governor Evans, and Evans had a right to share in decisions regarding the unit's makeup and training. For all of these reasons, and not for politics, Chivington said, he had made the Denver trip.[8] There is no record of Curtis's reaction to Chivington's defense, but perhaps the general was convinced of its accuracy; there was no further suggestion that the colonel was doing anything improper.

At about this time, Curtis appeared to have some second thoughts about whether the Cheyennes were waging war against white settlers in Colorado. Shortly after his face-to-face confrontation with Chivington, Curtis told several junior officers of his conviction that almost all Native groups in the territory were participating in "vicious and continuous" attacks against whites. He specifically blamed the Cheyennes for the continuing raids, but said there was also "ample evidence" that the Cheyennes were aided by large numbers of Arapaho, Comanche, and Kiowa warriors. Curtis said that only an all-out effort on the part of his troops could put down the insurrection.

But just as Curtis started to concentrate on the Indian troubles in Colorado, his Civil War responsibilities forced him to change his focus. Confederate troops again invaded Missouri, and were threatening to sweep through the state, and on into southeastern Kansas. The War Department ordered General Curtis to respond quickly to this new Southern threat, giving it his "personal and highest priority attention;" that meant the Indian war was once again on the back burner. Before leaving for Missouri, Curtis appointed General James G. Blunt to take over the anti–Indian command.

General Blunt was in his middle thirties, and in private life had been a Kansas physician. Grossly overweight, his irreverent troops knew him as "fat boy." He had been active in the underground railroad, helping slaves escape from the South, in the years prior to the War. He had no experience as an officer, but was a close friend and supporter of Kansas Senator James M. Lane, who had helped Blunt win his commission. Some sources suggest that Blunt was a womanizer, and that he used foul language "as a matter of course."[9]

Before departing the frontier, General Curtis confided to General Blunt that he found the Indians in Colorado far more hostile than he had previously supposed. He said it would be a good idea to implement Evans' plan to separate friendly groups from unfriendly ones, and then "vigorously pursue" those who were hostile.[10]

Wednesday, July 27. The situation in Colorado had become so critical that Governor Evans issued another proclamation—his third since early June. This one was an executive order prohibiting any wagon of any description, any wagon train, or any individual from leaving Denver for any point to the east or north of the city. Wagon trains were permitted to leave the city heading south or west, providing they had written permission from the governor, and "providing they understand the perils of such a trip." The order urged all whites living on the plains to come to Denver for their own protection from the "continuing murderous rampages by the redskins."

Saturday, July 30. An army patrol from the Eleventh Kansas Cavalry set out to search the Smoky Hill Country for hostile Indians. After more than a week without seeing any Indians whatsoever, they returned to Salina on Sunday, August 7—and were immediately attacked by approximately 300 warriors. The attackers were repulsed, but only after they had wounded three soldiers and had run off all horses at the post.

Tuesday, August 9. An army patrol found four buffalo hunters, killed with arrows and then scalped, at Beaver Creek, Kansas—about forty miles northwest of Salina.

Thursday, August 11. Cheyenne and Sioux warriors attacked two large wagon trains near the Plum Creek relay station. Approximately 100 Cheyenne Dog Solders surrounded the wagon trains, killed sixteen men, kidnapped three women and two children,[11] stole the goods, drove off the animals, and burned the wagons. A teamster, who survived the attack by hiding in a ditch, said there was no question that the attackers were Dog Soldiers.

Monday, August 15. The ranch of Frederick Smith, on the Colorado–Kansas border, was attacked. The warriors burned the buildings, murdered the hired man, and stole all the horses and steers.

In light of these continuing attacks, scores of people now abandoned their ranches and fled to the nearest army fort for protection. Some of them waited too long to begin the journey. One family of six was murdered and scalped within a half-mile of Fort Kearney, Nebraska. A small village on Nebraska's Little Blue River was burned to the ground; the seven residents of the community were never accounted for.

Notes

1. Alvin Josephy, *The Civil War in the American West* (Alfred A. Knopf, New York, NY, 1991), 104.
2. Ibid., 108.
3. David Berthrong, *The Southern Cheyennes* (University of Oklahoma Press, 1975), 192–3.
4. *Rocky Mountain News*, June 25, 1864.
5. *The Civil War in the American West*, 307.
6. Ibid., 306.
7. Ibid., 308.
8. *The Southern Cheyennes*, 192.
9. *The Civil War in the American West*, 351.

10. *The Southern Cheyennes*, 195.
11. *The Southern Cheyennes*, 199, says that four women and a baby girl were kidnapped in this raid; all other sources consulted placed the number as given here.

–SEVEN–

Six Weeks of Crisis

VERY DAY brought three or four new reports of attacks, murders, kidnappings, and horse or cattle thefts. By the second week of August, the entire Great Plains was tightly in the grip of terror. The reports took a long time to reach authorities; mail coaches no longer ran, nor were ordinary stagecoaches, emigrant wagon trains, or other travelers on the roads. Telegraph wires were down most of the time, having been cut or pulled down by Indians. When telegraph service was restored, the wires hummed with new reports of atrocities. Simply moving around outside a city was highly risky; only a few persons dared travel at all. Those who did generally traveled in heavily armed groups, and rode horseback, so as not to be encumbered with any heavy loads.

Monday, August 8, 1864. Colonel William Collins, commander at Fort Laramie, decided that the continuous and worsening attacks made it far too dangerous for his wife, Catherine Weber Collins, to

Courtesy Colorado Historical Society

COLONEL WILLIAM O. COLLINS

As commander of Fort Laramie, this lawyer–turned–soldier was considered one of the calmer and more rational army leaders. He was Chivington's superior, and frequently relayed orders to "get tough" on Indians.

remain with him at the Wyoming outpost. He arranged for her to head back East until things cooled down.

One day later, the stagecoach carrying Mrs. Collins and her eight-year-old niece, Florence, reached the northeastern Colorado community of Julesburg. Mrs. Collins wrote in her diary:

> We arrived in Julesburg this morning. [Because there was no sign of trouble here] the escort of men who accompanied us to our encampment started back to Fort Laramie....and behold! When we got here General Mitchell learned by telegraph that Indians had attacked and burned a wagon train yesterday at the Bluffs Canyon near Plum Creek Station [near present day Lexington, Nebraska], killing eleven emigrants, plundering and burning their wagons and taking as captive two or three women and children. It seems as if there is to be a general Indian war which will lead to the extermination of this race along this great thoroughfare....In the event of an Indian attack [against the stage coach], we were to lie down flat on the ground as soon as the wagons were corralled, so the [rifle] balls would pass over us.[1]

Also on the eighth of August, Lieutenant J. Boone telegraphed a message to Colonel Summers at Fort Kearney, Nebraska, telling him, "Send company of men here quick as God can send them; 100 Indians in sight, firing on ox train."[2] General Mitchell replied, "Major George O'Brien en route your assistance. Make no delay if possible. Overtake the devils and take no prisoners."[3] That same day, a village of farmers near Liberty relay station (near the present-day community of Oak, Nebraska), was attacked. Every man in the village was killed. Mrs. William Eubanks, Junior; her four-year-old daughter, Isabelle (called Belle); her infant son; and sixteen-year-old Laura Wilbur were captured and carried away by the Indians.

When the teenager was released some time later, she said she had been kidnapped by Cheyenne and Arapaho braves. Laura said "after they had their way with me," she was traded for five ponies to Arapaho chief Neva. This apparently was the same chief who told the army that it was "definitely" Cheyenne Dog Soldiers, under the leadership of Roman Nose, who had murdered the Hungate family.

Mrs. Snyder, another woman who was kidnapped at about the same time, could not endure the degradation and shame of the constant debasement by her captors; she killed herself two days after being abducted. Several other white women prisoners were eventually released, after Major Edward Wynkoop negotiated with the Indians holding them captive.

There is confusion as to whether the kidnapped children belonged to Mrs. Eubanks or to Mrs. Laura Roper. Newspaper accounts which apparently refer to the same incident, indicate the children were Mrs. Ropers'. A Denver newspaper, interviewed Mrs. Molly Sanford, one of the women with whom Mrs. Roper stayed following her release from captivity:

> There were some prisoners ransomed by Colonel Wynkoop from the Indians—Laura Roper and two children. I had taken them at my home for a while. Mrs. Roper was subjected to all the indignities given to white women, and the children were brutally treated by the squaws. The mother was taken away and the poor girl left. She saw her father butchered, and although only three years old, can and does recount the whole tragedy.
>
> I took her, thinking I might adopt her, but I could not stand it. She would wake up from a sound sleep, sit up in bed with staring eyes, and go into detail over the

whole thing. She was scarred all over her body with prints of arrow points the squaws had tortured her with. Mrs. Roper, her mother, died later in Kansas, but we were never able to learn what happened to little Belle.[4]

Tuesday, August 9. Indians chased a white soldier back inside Fort Lyon after he stepped outside the gates to look for a stray horse. A few hours later, a fifteen-man detachment from Fort Lyon battled an estimated 200 warriors only a quarter mile from the front gate of the post, wounding two braves before retreating back behind the walls. Army records do not mention possible casualties among the soldiers.

Later the same day, a small wagon train was attacked seven miles east of Fort Lyon. Two travelers were killed and scalped, and two others wounded. The Indians looted the wagons, burned them, and drove off the animals.

Major Wynkoop, the officer in command at Fort Lyon, sent word to Colonel Chivington that "at least one thousand hostile Indians" were operating in the immediate area. There were so many, he said, that his relative handful of soldiers dared not even venture outside the fort or they would "certainly be killed and scalped."

Indian Agent Colley agreed with that frightening assessment, and went to Fort Lyon for his own protection. In spite of his generally favorable history of contact with the Indians, Colley was now afraid to venture outside the walls of the fort.

Wednesday, August 10. Two civilians, riding between buildings just outside the walls of Fort Lyon, were killed and scalped. At about the same time, several Indians attacked another small military detachment about a mile north of Fort Lyon, but the soldiers formed a circle and were able to drive off the attackers. Two of the assailants were killed before the others fled. The dead were identified as Cheyenne Dog Soldiers.

On the same afternoon, an estimated 100 braves attacked a wagon train a mile southwest of Fort Cottonwood, Nebraska. All of the eight people with the train were killed and scalped.

Still on the same day, a family of seven was murdered and scalped five miles west of Fort Cottonwood, and two travelers, on the main trail eight miles east of the fort, were shot from their saddles and scalped.

Thursday, August 11. Governor Evans again sent friendly Indians to visit all the Indian camps and tribes they could find. They carried the message that those who wished to avoid open warfare with the white man must gather at Forts Lyon, Larned, and Laramie, or Camp Collins "without delay." He renewed his warning that Indians encountered away from those posts would henceforth be considered hostile and at war with whites. The warning this time was quite blunt: if you are not camped at one of the specified forts, you will be killed.

On that same afternoon, Evans issued a new proclamation to the white population of Colorado. Evans said the territory was now under a "virtual state of siege," and called on citizens of the territory to "kill and destroy, as enemies of the country, wherever they may be found, all hostile Indians."[5]

Off the record, Evans confided to close advisors that the situation might be even more critical than most people supposed. There were simply too few troops in the territory to put a stop the deadly, and increasingly frequent, Indian raids, and no more troops would be available in the near future because of the Civil War. What few soldiers were still assigned to the prairie were doing their best, but they were too few and too scattered to be effective. In many cases, they were so few that they dared not even venture outside the protective walls of their forts, lest they be wiped out by Indian attackers.

In desperation, Evans telegraphed the Department of War, pleading for the return to Denver of all Colorado men currently in uniform, because they "must be free to defend their own families from this real and immediate threat."[6] He got no answer to the wire, nor did he expect to; he confided to aides that since Washington never bothered to reply to his appeals, such telegrams were sent mostly to make local citizens feel as if efforts were being made on their behalf.

Friday, August 12. Eighty covered wagons were gathered at the Little Blue relay station on the Nebraska–Wyoming border, ninety miles northeast of Denver, awaiting an army escort to Fort Laramie. About 150 Indians attacked the train, but were driven away in a five-hour battle. During the fierce fighting, nine men were killed, and about seventy-five horses and mules were driven off.

Two hours after the Indians withdrew from the wagon train, the nearby ranch home of William Kettredge was raided. Two people were killed and scalped, all of the buildings burned, and all of the livestock were run off.

Sunday, August 14. At long last, Governor Evans received a telegram from Washington, appropriating funds to officially raise a regiment of "mounted, 100 day's men" for the defense of Colorado. Prior to that time, such a unit was "authorized" but not funded—

ATTENTION!
INDIAN
FIGHTERS

Having been authorized by the Governor to raise a
Company of 100 day

U. S. VOL CAVALRY!

For immediate service against hostile Indians. I call upon all who wish to engage in such
service to call at my office and enroll their names immediately.

Pay and Rations the same as other U. S.
Volunteer Cavalry.

Parties furnishing their own horses will receive 40c per day, and rations for the same,
while in the service.
The Company will also be entitled to all horses and other plunder taken from the Indians.

Office first door East of Recorder's Office.

HAL SAYR.

Central City, Aug. 13, '64.

Courtesy Colorado Historical Society

**RECRUITING POSTER FOR THIRD COLORADO
VOLUNTEERS**

meaning that nothing could actually be done to begin
the recruiting and training.

While Evans was still reading the long-awaited
wire, a messenger arrived with news that 400 Ute

warriors were on their way down from the mountains, apparently planning to attack the Plains Indians. The Ute war party presumably was aiming at their traditional enemies—the Cheyennes, Arapahos, and Kiowas. Evans ordered that "no one must interfere" with the Utes, adding, "If these red rebels can be killed off by one another, it will be a great savings to the government, for I am fully satisfied that to kill them is the only way to have peace and quiet." According to some sources, Evans said that killing off of all hostile Indians was the only way Colorado would ever finally become a state.[7]

On that same day, about 100 miles northeast of Denver, a combined unit of 150 soldiers from the Seventh Iowa Cavalry and the First Nebraska Volunteers started out from the Little Blue stagecoach station to check area ranches. The soldiers had gone less than a mile, when they were attacked by a party of warriors, variously estimated to be from 250 to 500 in number. The soldiers had a howitzer with them, but the weapon immediately broke down and the troops beat a hasty retreat back inside the fort.

Monday, August 15. The Overland Stage Coach Company reported that one of its stages, traveling from Fort Leavenworth, Kansas to Denver, had vanished somewhere between Julesburg and Latham Station (just east of Greeley). The coach and its five occupants were never located.

That same day, bands of Indians were reported looting and burning ranches within thirty miles of Denver. Panic-stricken ranchers and their families fled into the city, abandoning their drought-ravaged crops and their animals.

Governor Evans telegraphed another message to General Samuel Curtis, telling him that Colorado's situation was desperate. With all roads into Denver cut off, and local farmers abandoning their crops, the governor feared that all the citizens of Colorado "might well starve to death in the near future." Although the Third Colorado Volunteers were now being trained, Evans said they were not yet ready for battle, nor would they ever be strong enough to protect the entire territory. He pleaded with Curtis to send regular army troops to defend Colorado.

Replying on behalf of General Curtis, General William Rosecrans telegraphed his regret that no troops could be spared, because of yet another anticipated Confederate attack into southern Missouri (and possibly southeastern Kansas.)

Those were the last telegrams into or out of Denver for more than two weeks. The wires went dead on Sunday evening, August 15, and service was not restored until August 30. During that time, Denver was totally isolated. The city (and territory) was desperately short of food and remained on rationing; martial law kept most stores and all bars closed. Civilians walked the streets of Denver carrying shotguns, rifles, and pistols.

Out in Colorado's Arkansas River valley, George Bent decided at last to end any pretense as to his intentions. Ignoring the advice of his father, Bent left his father's home and joined his brother, Charles in living with Chief Black Kettle's tribe of Cheyennes. According to author David Lavender, George decided to begin living with the Indians because, "the taste of excitement had been too fresh on his tongue for the quiet of the Purgatory ranch to hold him, and on the Solomon he found the turmoil he wanted."[8] Also, Bent's mother was

Owl Woman, a full-blooded Cheyenne, who lived with Black Kettle's people.

Within a few days, George Bent had a falling out with tribal elders. He left Black Kettle's village to join the Dog Soldiers of Chief Roman Nose, and was said to have been with a Cheyenne war party that killed and scalped two Delaware Indians in late August.

Monday, August 15. Two Cheyenne warriors warned rancher Eldridge Gerry and his wife (who was Cheyenne) to take everything of value and go quickly to Denver, because "800 to 1000 Cheyenne, Arapaho, Kiowa, Kiowa-Apache, and Comanche warriors intend to sweep the south Platte valley clean of whites." They told him that the older chiefs had now completely lost control of young warriors, who were fully committed to a fight-to-the-death war. If possible, the young militants planned to drive all settlers from the prairie; if they fought back, the Indians at least wanted to kill as many as possible before being killed. Gerry and his wife hastened into town to warn the citizens of Denver.

Because the telegraph lines were down, Governor Evans dispatched military messengers to Fort Laramie to sound the warning. The lines out of Fort Laramie were still intact, and the base commander wired Secretary of War Edwin Stanton that there was now "unlimited information" from multiple sources that all the plains Indians were at war with the white man.

Tuesday, August 16. Ben Eaton (who later became the governor of Colorado) and his bride had been living in a tent near the community of Windsor, preparing to build a home on land they had claimed. Because of the danger, Eaton took his wife to Camp Collins for safety.[9]

Wednesday, August 17. Governor Evans increased the scope of martial law in Colorado, "due to the Indian emergency." The proclamation included a stiff curfew, the closure of most businesses, and a prohibition against all travel east of Denver.

Thursday, August 18. Retired Union Army General Fitz-Hugh Porter arrived in Denver from his gold claim in the mountains, near Fairplay. He insisted that Governor Evans permit him to recruit an army of volunteers, from among the out-of-work miners, to go on the offensive against hostile Indians. Governor Evans politely declined the offer, saying that Colonel Chivington was in charge of training and leading Colorado volunteers.

Between August 22 and August 29, Indians wiped out three wagon trains on the Santa Fe Trail in southeastern Colorado. Eleven white men were killed and scalped in attacks, the wagons looted and burned, and the animals stolen. Two white trappers were captured, brutally tortured, killed, and scalped within sight of Fort Lyon; there were so many warriors involved that the soldiers dared not ride out and try to rescue the hapless victims.

Another wagon train was wiped out on the upper Cimmaron River. Three Mexican teamsters with the wagon train were captured, but spared because of their nationality. Five white men with the train were tortured, killed, and mutilated. Army reports said five men were decapitated, and their hearts cut out. One of the Mexican survivors said the Indians held a celebration, dancing around the bodies of the victims and kicking their heads across the prairie.[10]

As September arrived, there finally was some good news. The Confederate threat to drive into Kansas had been blunted, and Southern soldiers were again retreating toward Arkansas. General Curtis pulled several units off the Civil War front line, and hastened them westward to try to relieve beleaguered Colorado. One large unit of 628 soldiers, accompanied by five mountain howitzers and three dozen Pawnee scouts, were sent by Curtis to sweep across western Kansas. Their task was to secure roads there, and try to restore communication with Denver.

The soldiers quickly rode through the Smoky Hill valley, which they considered the most likely trouble spot—and found no sign of difficulty. On Wednesday, September 7, they divided into two groups; General Robert Mitchell took 400 of the men northwestward toward Fort Cottonwood, Nebraska, while General Curtis led the smaller group southwestward toward Fort Riley, Kansas.

When he arrived at Fort Riley, Curtis was told that Confederates had counterattacked, and had broken through Yankee defenses in southern Missouri. The rebels were rapidly sweeping northward and westward. Once again, the Civil War took precedence over the Indian war; General Curtis and his men left immediately for the front lines in Missouri.

Before departing Fort Riley, the weary Curtis hastily penned a letter to Governor Evans, saying that based on his observations the threat from Indians had been grossly overstated. Apparently disregarding the fact that he had only been in western Kansas, and most of the reported attacks were now in central Colorado, Curtis reported that he had personally found no hostile Indians. It appeared to him, he said, that settlers could easily defend themselves from "those few trouble-makers" who were still around.

Friday, September 9. Major George Wynkoop, commander at Fort Lyon, and BIA Agent Colley each received a hand-delivered letter from George Bent. Claiming the authorization of several Cheyenne chiefs to write the letter, Bent said the Cheyennes were ready to exchange unspecified white prisoners for several Indians who were being held in various army stockades. The letter expressed the Cheyennes' desire to see restoration of peace for all Indians and whites. The letter admitted that "several" war parties were out hunting whites, but that other Indians expected to contact them soon. The implication was that once the warring groups were contacted, they would cease hostilities.

Major Wynkoop dutifully sent a messenger to pass along the letter to Colonel Chivington, but expressed doubt as to the letter's truthfulness; the letter came a few hours after he received reports on the latest string of Indian attacks.

Then Wynkoop seized the two Indian warriors who had brought him Bent's letter—Minimic and One Eye—ordering them to lead him and his troops back to George Bent and the other hostile Indians. This action by Wynkoop would be another key element in the awful bloodshed that followed.

There is ample evidence that Wynkoop was a good officer and soldier when sober, but he had developed the habit of hitting the bottle each evening. Men under his command later testified that for extended periods of time each night, virtually no one was in charge because of Wynkoop's drunken stupor. And Wynkoop apparently took a supply of rot gut whiskey with him on this campaign.

Guided by his Indian captives, Wynkoop took 130 soldiers and two mountain howitzers northward into central Colorado. Within hours, he came to a huge Cheyenne village containing 600 to 800 Cheyenne warriors, most of them Dog Soldiers. He was surprised to find the "moderate" Cheyenne chief Black Kettle in the camp. Wynkoop ordered his men to make camp, and requested a meeting with the Indian leaders—which was granted. Many of the soldiers would later claim that the bottle was passed around at this leadership conference.

While they were talking, hundreds of Indian warriors surrounded the soldiers. The camp site selected by Wynkoop was terrible, from a military point of view. It was surrounded on three sides by a creek. The opposite banks were higher than the camp site, and were covered with underbrush. Within hours, angry Indian warriors had not only surrounded the soldiers, but had even taken control of a howitzer. Chief Black Kettle eventually ordered the braves to pull back, but they stayed in sight of the soldiers, and always displayed their weapons.

Eventually, the Indians set fire to grass in a location where the evening breeze would sweep the fire into the soldier's camp. The fire forced a temporary break-up of the conference while the army pulled back about twelve miles. When Major Wynkoop and his top officers went back into council with the Indians, they remained there for two days. During that time, the soldiers were constantly surrounded, and felt threatened by the hundreds of warriors.

In later written and sworn testimony, Sergeant B. N. Forbes, Company D, First Colorado Cavalry, gave his version of what happened:

> After going into camp on the Smoky Hill, Major
> Wynkoop and the officers held a consultation with the

chiefs. We remained in this camp about six hours. The
Indians came into this camp, about five Indians to one
white man. The Indians were all armed. They took
from us our provisions, also the wagon, forcibly. The
Indians behaved towards the troops pretty saucily. A
few that could talk English used pretty hard words.
Looking at the troops they said, 'Damn you', etc. They
kept the troops guarded; when a soldier got up and left
his place, two or three Indians would follow him.
Whether this was intentionally I could not say, it
looked like it, although they had their bows strung all
the time and arrows in their hands. Quite a number of
Indians also surrounded the cannon; Captain Hardy
went to one of their chiefs, Black Kettle, and got him
to talk to the Indians and coax them away; they
saddled up their ponies and went away, first setting
fire to the grass to the windward of our camp, which
compelled us to break camp and move back about 10
or 15 miles, where we camped that night. The camp in
which these things occurred was made right in the
bend of a creek, encircling it on three sides. The
opposite bank of the creek that encircled us was
covered with a thick undergrowth, the bank being
very favorable for the concealment of the enemy.
Generally the camp was arranged very poorly for
defense. I think the creek, etc., furnished a fine
ambuscade for the enemy. I was sergeant of the guard
that day and did not receive orders from any person,
Major Wynkoop or anyone else, to keep the Indians
out of camp. In the camp to which we moved, 10 or 15
miles distant, we remained two nights, and one day
one of the Indians that was with us left us, which
allowed some excitement in the minds of the troops,
and there was strong talk among the men of breaking
camp and returning to Fort Lyon with orders. There
was talk among the men that there was more whiskey
aboard the outfit than was necessary. Some said they
had confidence in their officers when they were sober,
but did not like to trust themselves among the Indians
among them when they believed they were drinking.[11]

Black Kettle and other chiefs told Wynkoop that the older Indians wanted peace, but that young warriors— including the young warriors in this village—did not want peace. Black Kettle said the Dog Soldiers, especially, would not tolerate peace. Wynkoop asked Black Kettle to release all white prisoners in his custody to prove that he personally desired peace. Black Kettle never admitted he had any white prisoners, but did ask for time to confer privately with other leaders. The Indians withdrew to a point about a mile away and conferred for four hours before requesting another meeting with Wynkoop.

At this subsequent meeting, the Indians released four women and several small children. The women were Daniell Marble, who had been kidnapped from a ranch on the South Platte River near Greeley; and Laura Roper, Isabella Eubanks, and Ambrose Usher, abducted from a ranch on the Little Blue River along the Wyoming–Nebraska border. The women were in terrible shape; all had been brutally beaten and repeatedly raped, and the little children bore scars from repeated torturing. Chief Black Kettle told Major Wynkoop that there were numerous prisoners in various Cheyenne villages, and said he hoped more could be released in the future.

As the conference ended, Wynkoop wasn't sure whether he had accomplished anything meaningful— other than freeing the captives. He was not, after all, authorized to speak or negotiate for the government or the army; they didn't even know he was meeting with the Cheyennes. And Black Kettle made it clear he was speaking only for himself and a few older Indians, and warned repeatedly that many Cheyennes still wanted war.

Notes

1. Ruth Dunn, "Attack on Black Kettle's Village," Unpublished Notes, Heritage Collection, Lincoln, Nebraska Public Library, 8–9.
2. Ibid., 9.
3. Ibid., 9.
4. Ibid., 9–11.
5. David Berthrong, *The Southern Cheyennes* (University of Oklahoma Press, 1975), 192–3.
6. Alvin Josephy, *The Civil War in the American West* (Alfred A. Knopf, New York, 1991), 306.
7. It should be noted that white citizens of Colorado were deeply divided over whether to apply for statehood. Governor Evans and Colonel Chivington were the spokesmen for the pro–statehood Republican party, and they were supported by the *Rocky Mountain News* publisher, Bill Byers. The anti–statehood faction was also powerful, and had so far been successfully encouraging Congress to delay consideration of statehood for the territory.
8. David Lavender, *Bent's Fort* (University of Nebraska Press, Lincoln/London, 1972), 375.
9. *The Southern Cheyennes*, 203.
10. Ibid, 205.
11. John Chivington, *To the People of Colorado: Synopsis of the Sand Creek Investigation,* (Wagner-Camp, Denver, June, 1865), 12–13.

–EIGHT–

The Eve of Tragedy

SATURDAY, SEPTEMBER 17, 1864. Colonel John Chivington telegraphed the War Department, asking that Colorado be given preference for a shipment of arms and ammunition being prepared for troops at Fort Union, New Mexico. Chivington pointed out that in New Mexico the arms would merely strengthen an existing stockpile, for use in the event of trouble. Colorado needed the weapons immediately for self defense from a murderous enemy. Chivington's wire claimed that 3,000 Indians were already gathered in the general vicinity of Fort Lyon. He said no one could tell for sure which of those were hostile and which were friendly, but recent events and common sense dictated that precautions be taken.

Sunday, September 18. General Blunt was still exploring northeastern Colorado when he stumbled across a large Indian encampment on Walnut Creek. Unable to determine whether the people in camp were friendly or hostile, Blunt halted the main body of troops several miles from the village. He then ordered Major

Scott J. Anthony to take a handful of soldiers from the First Colorado Volunteers, ride on into the village, and "there to determine the attitude of the occupants."

Anthony rode to within a hundred yards of the village, then stopped his unit. While most of the men stayed put, Anthony and two enlisted men moved cautiously toward the tepees.

In a flash Anthony found himself surrounded by Cheyenne warriors apparently numbering several hundred. What really happened in the ensuing minutes will always be in question, since the two sides tell sharply different stories.

Someone fired a shot, and then everyone was firing shots. As the hundreds of warriors began advancing toward Blunt's command, the untested soldiers appeared on the verge of panic. Two Pawnee scouts with Blunt may have prevented a full-blown rout; they shouted at the green soldiers to dismount and dig in. The soldiers did so and subsequently were able to hold the Cheyennes at bay.

General Blunt and the main body of soldiers had begun moving leisurely toward the village, unaware of the outbreak of gunfire. As Blunt topped a ridge a mile or so from the village, he saw the flashes from the muzzles of many guns, and recognized at once what was happening. Blunt ordered his remaining troops to charge, and about 300 soldiers raced forward. The Cheyennes saw the attack coming, broke off the engagement and fled. They left nine dead on the battlefield, and Anthony believed several others were carried away by the retreating warriors. Anthony suffered two dead and eleven wounded.

Blunt's men pursued the Indians for several miles. They were astounded a short time later when scouts determined that they were not following just a few hundred warriors as they had supposed, but rather were on the trail of several thousand Indians, apparently including many women and children. Evidence found in the area later indicated as many as 4,000 may have been camped in the immediate area of the gun battle. Of that number, about 1,500 were probably warriors. Recognizing that he was in no position to battle so many of the enemy, Blunt halted the pursuit and withdrew from the area.[1]

Tuesday, September 27. Returning to Fort Lyon, General Blunt telegraphed both General Curtis and Governor Evans to report what he had found. He warned that the 1,500 warriors he had personally encountered were "clearly and obviously" hostile, "...as evidenced by the attack they launched against my troops."

No white person in Colorado doubted that there was an all-out war with the Indians, or that there was great and mounting danger of being overrun by "hostile savages" at any moment. The thought must have struck terror into the hearts of the white population, knowing what warriors traditionally did to their enemies— including torture, rape, enslavement, and murder.

Sunday, September 25. The Reverend William Crawford, a circuit-riding preacher representing the American Home Missionaries, wrote a letter from his Denver office to his headquarters in Illinois. His letter probably represented the thoughts and feelings of most whites then living in Colorado. In part the letter said:

> We are now at open war with nearly all the Indians on the plains—the Sioux, the Cheyenne, Kiowa, Arapaho and Comanche. General Curtis with a considerable

force is marching toward the Blue River and a regiment of 100-day men is in Denver awaiting orders. Other companies are out on the plains. The Indians avoid open battle and only fall upon little parties of emigrants and unprotected ranches. The loss they have caused in life and property cannot well be estimated.

For friends concerned about our safety, rest assured that we can defend ourselves against attack. There is one sentiment in regard to the disposition of the Indians; let them be exterminated, men, women and children. They are regarded as a race accursed like the ancient Canaanites, devoted of the Almighty to utter destruction. I do not share these views, but my feelings have changed. The grace of God may be sufficient for them, but humanly speaking, there seems no better destiny ahead than to fade away before the white man.[2]

Wednesday, September 28. Major Wynkoop arrived unexpectedly in Denver, accompanied by seven well-known Cheyenne chiefs. Among the group were Black Kettle, White Antelope, and Bull Bear, all of whom wielded great influence over southern Cheyennes. Major Wynkoop said he had been talking to these chiefs near Fort Lyon, and believed they now honestly sought to negotiate peace. He also reported for the first time that these chiefs had released to his custody four women they had been holding captive for weeks. He said the Cheyennes already camped around Fort Lyon appeared ready to release additional captives.

Wynkoop was undoubtedly proud of himself for successfully negotiating freedom for the women and for bringing the Cheyenne leaders into Denver for peace talks. He must have been stunned, then—and perhaps even a little embarrassed—at the response he received.

The initial reaction from both Governor Evans and Colonel Chivington was outrage when they learned the

Courtesy Colorado Historical Society

BLACK KETTLE, CHEYENNE CHIEF

Admittedly unable to control the young braves of his tribe, Black Kettle spoke eloquently in favor of peace, but frequently participated in bloody attacks on whites. He admitted holding several white women and children as prisoners.

battered condition of the released women. They also were angry because these same "peace chiefs" were apparently leaders of the bands that in recent days had fought pitched battles with General Blunt and other soldiers. Nonetheless, Evans and Chivington agreed to "council" with the chiefs.

When the meeting was convened a short time later, Evans and Chivington were accompanied by George L. Shoup, BIA Agent Simeon Whitley, and fur trader John S. Smith, who served as the official interpreter. He apparently was the only white man in the room who spoke or understood their language; it would later be felt that this may have been a serious error. Records indicate that Bill Byers, publisher of the *Rocky Mountain News,* may also have sat in on the meeting as an unofficial observer, although that cannot be confirmed.

In the course of the peace conference, the Cheyenne leaders admitted that their warriors had been engaging in open warfare against whites, and that the war, in fact, was still underway. Black Kettle further admitted he knew of at least two additional women and one infant who were being held as prisoners in a Cheyenne village not far from Fort Lyon. One of the government representatives asked why the prisoners had not already been released, and one of the chiefs—it is not recorded which one—responded that it was because the women were being held by Dog Soldiers, over whom these "peace chiefs" had no control.

Under continued questioning from Evans and Chivington, White Antelope and Black Kettle confessed that in truth they no longer had any control whatsoever over any of the young warriors of their tribes, and further, that they could not speak for younger men at this meeting. However, the chiefs promised that if these talks went well they would do everything in their power to convince the young braves to stop the war against whites. They also promised to turn the young "trouble makers" over to white authorities.

As the questioning continued, Governor Evans seemed to conclude that the conference was essentially meaningless; the chiefs were able only to say that older Indians desired peace, but admitted they had no influence over young warriors and no authority to negotiate for them. At last the impatient governor bluntly told the chief that they had nothing to offer, and that further talks were useless unless the chiefs could control all warriors. And the governor added that until the chiefs spoke for everyone—including the Dog Soldiers—it would not be possible to declare any truce since it would be impossible to determine which Cheyennes were friendly and which were still at war.

One of the chiefs—again history does not say which one—responded that the specific incidents to which Evans had referred (even those involving attacks on wagon trains and ranchers) were merely misunderstandings. The chief said that most of the recent fighting, including the battle involving Major Wynkoop's troops, occurred when soldiers first attacked braves who were merely trying to return some horses that had been stolen by "bad" Indians.

Chivington asked Major Wynkoop whether it was true that his soldiers had fired first. Wynkoop said no, and repeated the information already filed in his official report: the Indians had fired the first shot at soldiers who were merely trying to determine whether the village was peaceful.

Chief Black Kettle then spoke of the Hungate murders. He said it was not true that Cheyennes were guilty of the atrocity, but rather that the Hungates were murdered by Arapaho warriors under Chief Friday. He said that Friday was currently camped on the Poudre River near Camp Collins, as were the killers. Under further questioning, however, Black Kettle said all the Arapahos in question were actually Dog Soldiers, who were now living in the village of Cheyenne Dog Soldier Chief Roman Nose.

The talks continued for several hours, even though it was increasingly apparent that the deliberations were totally meaningless. The army representatives apparently believed the chiefs were not telling the truth most of the time, and were refusing to accept any responsibility for the murders of more than 200 settlers over the past five weeks. Eventually, the chiefs also began to show signs of anger, impatience, and frustration.

Colonel Chivington, who had been sitting quietly during most of the meeting, was the last government representative to speak at the conference. Talking in a soft but firm voice, Chivington explained that he was not the final authority on matters involving the military, saying that his orders came from far away. But he carefully pointed out that the current instructions from his chief was to fight the Indians "until they lay down their arms in surrender." Then, summing up his position, Chivington added, "Only when all Indians give themselves up will we stop military action."[3]

By his statement, Chivington apparently meant to encourage them to go back to their villages and convince hostile young warriors that they must quit fighting or face continued—and losing—battles with the army. He was warning that until the warriors agreed to peace terms, all of their people remained subject to punitive action from the army. Chivington himself later said he was trying to impress upon the chiefs the fact that the army was prepared to wipe them out unless they quit waging war.

Later statements from tribal leaders who participated in the meeting indicate they interpreted (or may actually have been told by interpreter John Smith) that Chivington promised immediate peace to any Indian who surrendered to the soldiers. The Indian leaders said they understood that surrender could be accomplished by simply making camp at one of the forts in the area. The conflicting interpretation and language problem would become another key issue in the bitter dispute that was to follow.[4]

It is not clear whether anything might eventually have been accomplished had the talks continued. They were abruptly ended, however, by an angry outburst from Chief Bull Bear. While Governor Evans was in the midst of questioning White Antelope about attacks on specific ranches, Bull Bear suddenly leaped to his feet and proclaimed, "I am young. I can still fight. I have given my word to my brothers to fight with the whites. My brother Lean Bear died in trying to keep peace with the whites. I am willing to die fighting the whites, and expect to do so!"

Some accounts of the meeting say Bull Bear and two or three other chiefs stormed out of the conference at this point although official government records contain no such information. However, the meeting did end almost immediately after Bull Bear had spoken with the two sides going their separate ways.

At the conclusion of the Denver conference, Chivington telegraphed a summary of the meeting to General Curtis. Chivington's wire, which is a matter of record, indicated he and the others believed that nothing of importance had been achieved by the talks. He reported that the seven Cheyenne chiefs had said

Courtesy Colorado Historical Society

BULL BEAR, CHEYENNE CHIEF

Considered to be one of the most powerful Cheyenne leaders. Although he held several white women and children as prisoners, Bull Bear attended the Denver Peace Talks to seek an end to hostilities. He later stormed out of the talks, vowing he would die fighting whites. He did so: Bull Bear died at Sand Creek.

they could not control young warriors who continued to wage war on whites, and said that in keeping with General Curtis' instructions he had warned the chiefs that until all Indians surrendered they would all be hunted and killed by the army.

On a separate matter, Chivington reported to General Curtis that the Third Colorado Volunteers were now fully trained and ready for any assignment. However, Chivington said that with winter weather approaching, warring Indians were likely to cause less trouble and might even stop attacking altogether until the following spring; that had been their pattern in previous years. The colonel speculated that the peace overtures from the tribal leaders who had come to Denver might really have been prompted by the pending arrival of cooler weather.

General Curtis appears to have agreed with Chivington's assessment. He wired back that there could be no peace agreement until the ring leaders of the hostile warriors were brought to justice. The general's wire to his subordinate officer also made it clear that the Indians were to be "punished" and driven to their knees. The wire said in part, "I want no peace till the Indians suffer more....It is better to chastise [the Indians] before giving anything but a little to talk over."

The general's wire concluded with an order on which the entire Sand Creek dispute ultimately hinges: "No peace must be made without my direction."[5]

Thursday, September 29. Governor Evans wrote a letter to BIA agent Colley, saying the Denver "peace meeting" had produced no tangible results. He repeated to Colley that the only tribal groups in the territory considered to be at peace with whites at this time were those few Arapahos under Chief Friday, currently camped on the Poudre River (in northern Colorado, near Camp Collins). Evans repeated General Curtis's order that until Curtis personally gave specific permission otherwise, no one was to "make or accept peace" with any other Indians.

Evans then telegraphed essentially the same message to the new Commissioner of Indian Affairs, William Dole, in Washington. Dole subsequently wired back that since the Indians had declared war on the United States, only the United States Government could negotiate a peace with them. No negotiations were to be undertaken by any other entity, he said, and he reminded Governor Evans that the army was under orders to deal with the hostilities. Dole said Evans and the Colorado Territory must not intervene in the Federal affairs of the military.

This series of exchanges—especially Evans' comment that Chief Friday was at peace with whites— is somewhat surprising in light of the claims made by the seven Cheyenne chiefs. Just one day earlier they had told Evans that Chief Friday and his tribe of Arapaho warriors were responsible for the Hungate murders. Apparently Evans did not believe the Cheyennes and continued to be fully convinced that Roman Nose alone was to blame for the killings. Presumably the other white leaders agreed with that assessment.

Shortly after the fruitless peace talks in Denver, the *Rocky Mountain News* ran a front page editorial demanding "extermination of the red devils" who were making life miserable for local (white) citizens. The editorial suggested that the best thing that could happen to Colorado was for all the men in the territory to "take a few months off and dedicate that time to wiping out the Indians."

The tough editorial probably represented the viewpoint of most Coloradans, although an argument can be made that publisher Bill Byers probably had other motives for making such demands. Those who understood the workings of Colorado's most powerful men knew the editorial could also be a part of the frustration stemming from the political and financial implications of the continuing trouble. Byers had undertaken a personal campaign to publicize the grandeur of Denver and great investment opportunities offered in Colorado. Only two things could interfere with a huge influx of investments from the East: a perception that even the cities of Colorado were being overrun by hostile Indians, and a perception that the government had given away most of Colorado's most valuable land to the Native Americans (via earlier treaties).

The latter issue was an especially tough one for the pioneers and settlers of Colorado. They were repeatedly encouraged by the federal government to "go West" and settle the frontier. Several presidents had issued proclamations to make such settlement easier, and it was even considered patriotic to help the United States grow by civilizing the frontier. Yet every time a pioneer family tried to stake a claim to land in Colorado, they had to wade through a mountain of paperwork to determine whether the land technically belonged to the Indians as the result of some earlier treaty with one or more tribes.

The crux of the issue was not a moral right to use the land, but rather ownership of the legal title to the property. The Indian nations wanted the freedom to roam wherever they wanted, unrestricted by the white man's fences; the white man insisted on the right to enclose their land and contain their animals. The ongoing problem was discouraging growth and investment in Colorado, and was harmful to both the area's long-term financial prospects and the territory's chances of being granted statehood.

Publisher Byers knew that. Governor Evans knew it. Colonel Chivington knew it. And Chivington's anti–statehood enemies knew it!

Of course there is no question that the constant fighting posed real life-and-death dangers to everyone in Colorado. The settlers were up in arms, both literally and figuratively, over the continuing Indian raids. Commerce was at a virtual stand-still, with all roads into Denver now closed. Crucial merchandise was no longer being shipped to Denver. It was now not possible to get many of the goods required by farmers, ranchers, miners, and others. Three fourths of the gold mines in Colorado were shut down because of the drought or because they had broken-down machinery and could not get replacement parts due to this continuing "Indian trouble." Citizens were prohibited from traveling outside the cities. It was truly a grim situation.

A measure of the mood in the territory was evidenced by the large rewards which were being offered for the capture of those responsible for various atrocities. The reward for the killers of the Hungate family now totaled nearly $10,000.

Posters all over the Territory also offered a bounty for the scalp of any Indian. Ten dollars would be paid for the scalp of a squaw or a child, twenty dollars for a warrior: twenty-five dollars if the ears were still attached.

In their anger and frustration, the people of the West almost unanimously considered Indians to be something less than human beings; they were thought to be some lower form of life. It was this widely-held conviction that made it possible for posters to offer rewards for the scalps of women and children, and the so-called civilized whites not be offended by them.

The political savvy of John Chivington unquestionably sought to cash in on the local mood. As a great Civil War hero, leading military man of the territory, and brightly rising star of the Republican party, Chivington was frequently asked to speak to various civic groups. Like any good politician, he accepted as many such engagements as possible, and then told the people what they wanted to hear. And what they wanted to hear was toughly-worded rhetoric about the Indian menace.

Whether Chivington believed everything he is reported to have said is open to debate, given his theological background. Whenever Chivington demanded that the army quit talking and get on with a real war against the Indians, he was always met with a chorus of cheers; his words, after all, reflected the attitude of Colorado voters.

In late August, politician Chivington was reported to have told a civic banquet in Denver, "The Cheyennes will have to be soundly whipped—or completely wiped out—before they will be quiet. I say that if any of them are caught in your vicinity, the only thing to do is kill them. That is the only way."

In September, speaking at a gathering of deacons of the Methodist-Episcopal church, in which he was a pastor and elder, Chivington allegedly complained about the lack of action on the part of the army. He said, "It simply is not possible for Indians to obey or even understand any treaty. I am fully satisfied, gentlemen, that to kill them is the only way we will ever have peace and quiet in Colorado."

The later reports on this meeting claim that someone in the crowd asked Chivington whether he could solve the Indian problem if he were in charge.

According to the popular accounts of history, Chivington snapped, "Of course. I could run an empire if given the chance. The problem we have is that there are just too many people willing to sit around and do nothing while the trouble gets worse and worse. Give me the chance—and the manpower—and I can personally guarantee that the Indian problem will come to a quick end!"[6]

Monday, October 10. Colonel Chivington and the Third Colorado Volunteers were finally in the field, patrolling the vast prairie east of Denver. One scouting party of about forty men under the direct command of Captain David H. Nichols spotted a small Cheyenne village on a river bank a short distance ahead. Since by army and Territorial decree these were automatically considered to be enemies, Nichols quietly moved his troops into position above the village and then attacked. There is some indication that after a brief fight some people in the village may have tried to surrender, but it was too late. Six Indian men, three women, and a teenage boy were killed in the skirmish. A number of others apparently escaped.

When troops entered the Cheyenne village after the battle, Captain Nichols found an interesting collection of articles that seem typical of the difficulty in determining whether Indians were friend or foe. One of the recovered items was a framed certificate from Secretary of War Edwin Stanton, commending this particular group for their cooperation with white authorities. In the same tepee, however, Nichols found the fresh scalp of a white man, the blood-stained clothing of a white male, and freight bills taken from wagons that had been attacked and burned on the Overland trail more than a month earlier.[7]

Friday, October 14. An eight-man US Army patrol was riding along a road five miles from Plum Creek relay station when it was attacked by an estimated forty Cheyenne warriors. Two of the soldiers were killed and two others wounded, although the wounded men and four others managed to battle back to the station where the warriors broke off the attack. Among the survivors of this attack was Captain Henry Ribble, who reported that several dead braves were found on the battlefield after the attackers had withdrawn. He said the dead were positively identified as warriors from the tribe of Arapaho Chief White Antelope, who was one of the seven so-called peace chiefs.

On that afternoon Cheyenne "peace chief" Black Kettle and several lesser chiefs arrived at Fort Lyon, saying they wished to stop the fighting with whites. Major Wynkoop issued some food to them, and in keeping with Governor Evan's proclamation that Indians wishing peace must camp "at" the fort, told them they needed to stay close to Fort Lyon if they expected to be considered friendly. The chiefs complained that they must first return to the prairie to get the people of their villages and must thereafter be able to hunt to survive—but said they would return to Fort Lyon within a few days.

When General Curtis learned that Major Wynkoop had given food to the Indians and indicated the surrender would be accepted, he was furious. Such action was in direct violation of Curtis's previous orders that only he could negotiate a peace with, or accept surrender from, any of the Indians. He ordered that Major Wynkoop be immediately relieved of command and replaced by Major Scott J. Anthony. In addition, Curtis ordered Major B. C. Henning to have Major Anthony conduct an investigation to determine whether

Courtesy Smithsonian Institution

WHITE ANTELOPE, ARAPAHO CHIEF

Like Black Kettle, White Antelope spoke of peace but
regularly participated in raids on white settlers. Legend says
he died unarmed and as a martyr at Sand Creek—but sworn
testimony indicates he died attacking white soldiers.

Major Wynkoop "disobeyed orders, as rumored, by feeding and protecting hostile Indians." Major Henning is reported to have told Major Anthony to be careful in assuming command at Fort Lyon because "General Curtis will not permit or allow any agreement or treaty with the Indians without his approval, nor are you to allow any Indians to approach any [army] post on any excuse whatever."[8]

On the afternoon that Major Wynkoop was removed from command, Colonel Chivington's Third Colorado arrived at Bijou Basin about sixty miles east of Denver. They were operating under orders from General Curtis to begin a search at that point for hostile Indians operating in the area.

Wednesday, November 2. Some modern accounts of history say that Chief Left Hand, Chief Little Raven, and Chief Neva arrived at Fort Lyon, reporting they wished to surrender 650 of their people, and did not want war. In spite of the orders that he was not to make peace with anyone, these sources claim that Major Anthony apparently accepted the surrender. The warriors handed over their weapons, and released to the army a sizable herd of horses and mules taken in a series of earlier raids.

Major Anthony informed the surrendering Indians that they were considered to be prisoners of war, but said there was no room to hold them in the fort's little brig. He ordered them to camp within sight of the fort and await further orders, which they did. Anthony then telegraphed General Curtis's headquarters at Fort Leavenworth, asking for further instructions.

Sunday, November 6. Chief Black Kettle returned to Fort Lyon, telling Major Anthony that he wanted to

surrender more than 2,500 men, women, and children.
He asked for the same terms the Arapahos had received
a few days earlier. Major Anthony is reported to have
informed Black Kettle that the army was overwhelmed
by the sheer numbers of surrendering Indians, and said
that he had neither manpower nor authority, nor food
and supplies, to care for so many prisoners. He told
Black Kettle to stay close to Fort Lyon while he sought
instructions from Fort Leavenworth.

It is important to note that recorded history is
ambivalent over these reported surrenders and
conversations. In truth, it is difficult to know with any
degree of certainty which—if any—actually took place.

There is especially great confusion among
historians whether Major Anthony actually conferred in
person with Black Kettle, and whether he pointed out to
Black Kettle that the best camping ground in the area
to accommodate so many Indians was along Sand Creek,
thirty-five or forty miles northwest of Fort Lyon. A camp
which was so far away would hardly seem to be "at" a
fort, and would therefore seem to violate both common
sense and the terms for establishing the peace camps.

It would also seem strange that an army
commander under any circumstances would tell
surrendering enemies to camp more than a day's march
away from the nearest military unit. Such orders were
also significantly different than those orders known to
have been given a few days earlier by this same officer
when he had told the Arapahos that they must camp
"within sight" of Fort Lyon in order to have complied
with terms of surrender instructions.

Contrary to what most historians have recorded
about this incident, Major Anthony himself denies ever
having the recorded conversation with chief Black
Kettle. He argued in later sworn testimony that since

such a conversation would be similar to the agreement that got his predecessor in trouble with the commanding officer, Anthony clearly would not have acted as was later reported by the press.

Whether the conversation took place or not soon became a moot point. It is clear that thousands of Native Americans were suddenly descending on Fort Lyon and trying to surrender. The sheer numbers of those doing so made it impossible to keep everyone close to the fort. On the afternoon that some say Black Kettle tried to give up there, Major Anthony telegraphed General Curtis saying that possibly as many as 6,500 Indians were now camped in the immediate vicinity of the fort. He said all of them apparently wanted to make peace with the whites, and asked how he should proceed.

General Curtis was unmoved by this information. His return telegraph to Fort Lyon said only, "My previous orders stand!"[9]

Curtis dashed off another letter to Colonel Chivington. The letter said, in part, "Indians at war with us will be the object of our pursuit and destruction, but women and children will be spared."[10]

The letter—which Colonel Chivington said never reached him as he trooped across the prairie—made no mention of the several thousand Indians now gathered at Fort Lyon. Chivington, out of touch with both the army and the civilian government, continued to operate under his oft-repeated orders to "find and punish" hostile Indians.

Tuesday, November 15. Army General Patrick Connor arrived in Denver for consultations with territorial officials regarding the continuing attacks. The *Rocky Mountain News* quoted General Connor as telling Governor Evans, "There is no doubt that until the savages eastward of Denver shall have been thoroughly defeated and punished, no permanent peace can be hoped for, nor can their frequent raids upon the Overland Route be prevented by the number of troops at the disposal of the government."[11]

Wednesday, November 23. On Thanksgiving Eve, Governor Evans left Denver for Washington. The purpose of his trip was to seek additional arms and more soldiers to protect Coloradans from the continuing attacks.

In the afternoon, General Curtis wrote another letter to General Carlton, saying that some of the Indians in Colorado and Kansas apparently now genuinely wanted peace. He said, however, "there still remains some of these tribes and all of the Kiowas to attend to, and I have proposed a winter campaign" to wipe out the last of the hostile Indians.[12] Curtis noted that if the army's new winter campaign was to be successful it would have to be kept absolutely confidential and be well organized.

Perhaps most importantly, General Curtis told General Carlton that he would accept no surrender except from those tribes which had, "handed over all those members of their tribe guilty of the depredations, surrendered their captured livestock, released their prisoners, and laid down their arms."[13] All who read those orders interpreted them to mean that there could be no partial surrender by older members of a given tribe; surrender would only be acceptable if all the members of the tribe gave up and simultaneously ceased all hostilities.

General Curtis sent another telegram that afternoon to Major Henning at Fort Lyon. The wire said that a new, all-out campaign was being prepared against hostile Indians in Colorado and to assure its success, the march of all troops involved in the campaign were to be masked from the public. The commander also told Henning that Colonel Chivington was operating somewhere in the general vicinity of Fort Lyon, trying to locate hostile Indians who had recently attacked a wagon train in the area.

Finally, Curtis wrote a letter that day to Governor Evans, apparently unaware that Evans was now on his way to Washington. Curtis said he was at a loss as to what to do with those Arapahos and Cheyennes who were now camped at Fort Lyon and solicited ideas from the governor.

Sunday, November 27. Colonel Chivington arrived at Fort Lyon and conferred with Major Anthony. They talked at length about where the hostile Indians sought by Chivington might be camped, and about military plans for a new winter offensive. Major Anthony assigned 125 men from Fort Lyon to assist Chivington search for the hostile band he sought and to assure Chivington's success against those he considered to be extremely hostile.

Major Anthony and Colonel Chivington together studied maps of the area, and Anthony pointed out several locations where his scouts thought hostile Indians were camped.

Monday, November 28, 8:00 p.m. Armed with this intelligence from Major Anthony, Colonel Chivington departed Fort Lyon after dark. The unusual nighttime departure was to mask the movement of his troops in keeping with his instructions from General Curtis. Chivington was now accompanied by something over 700 men, including the 125 regulars on loan from Major

Anthony. He also had four twelve-pound mountain howitzers. Besides the army regulars and the Third Colorado, Chivington was accompanied by elements of the old First and Second Colorado Volunteers, who were on temporary duty as US soldiers, and assorted non-combatants such as doctors, veterinarians, teamsters and cooks.

Chivington's official report said later that his troops were guided that night by Robert Bent, the eldest son of William Bent and Owl Woman. Although Bent and others agreed that he was the guide, even this fact became an issue. Jim Beckwourth would later testify that it was he and not Bent who led the troops, but his testimony almost certainly was perjured; not a single person backed his claim. Bent was selected as guide because he supposedly knew exactly where the hostile Dog Soldiers were camped. Historians differ on whether Bent volunteered for the guide duty or was forced to lead Chivington's soldiers. However he was chosen, Bent apparently made a beeline for the village of Cheyenne chief Black Kettle.

Well before daylight the following morning, Chivington's soldiers had been led by Bent to the hills overlooking a large Cheyenne village on the banks of Sand Creek, forty miles from Fort Lyon. It remains debatable whether Bent or Chivington knew that among those in the village were two of Bent's brothers—former Confederate soldiers George and Charles—and Bent's youngest sister, Julia. Also there was Julia's husband, Ed Gurrier, a fur trapper who often supplied information of questionable accuracy to the army. Another trapper, John Smith (interpreter during the ill-fated Denver peace talks a short time earlier), was in the camp, as was his grown son.

After reaching Black Kettle's village the soldiers had to wait a short time for sunrise before attacking. There would later be testimony that because of the severe cold, many of the men drank whiskey for the remainder of the night in an effort to keep warm. There would also be testimony that by sunrise, some of the soldiers were actually drunk.[14]

Notes

1. Ruth Dunn, "Attack on Black Kettle's Village," Unpublished Notes, Heritage Collection, Lincoln, Nebraska Public Library, 8–11.

2. David Berthrong, *The Southern Cheyennes,* (University of Oklahoma Press, 1975), 207.

3. John Chivington, *To the People of Colorado: Synopsis of the Sand Creek Investigation* (Wagner–Camp, Denver, June, 1865), 14–15.

4. Summaries of this meeting and the remarks of participants are found in every major account of the Sand Creek Massacre. The information in *The Southern Cheyennes,* 197–215 is especially helpful and complete. It should be noted, however, that many writers, including respected authors such as Berthrong, make many unsupported assumptions about the motives of those participating in this conference. Berthrong asserts that the whites "refused Indian peace overtures" at this meeting, and says the refusal by Evans was because he wanted land cessions from the Indians "as much as he wanted peace". Berthrong says gaining title to the land would have helped Evans' drive for statehood by ending confusion over ownership. Berthrong also states that John Chivington felt that if he could achieve success as an Indian fighter, he would be perceived a hero and would be able to win his upcoming election for Congress whenever Colorado statehood was approved. There is no evidence whatsoever that these assumptions about how the men felt or about their private motives are accurate. No written record exists—including the diaries of Evans and Chivington—that would indicate any of these assumptions are correct; to the extent that either man addressed his personal thoughts and motives, they flatly contradict the common

assumptions of these later writers.

5. *The Southern Cheyennes*, 212.

6. The various comments attributed to Chivington speaking as a politician are contained in most histories of the era. However, like the often stated motives of John Chivington, there is reason to question the validity of these quotes. Chivington himself always denied having made most of the statements, and it eventually came down to his word against someone else's whether he actually said what was quoted. (See footnote #14.)

7. *The Southern Cheyennes*, 213.

8. Ibid., 215.

9. Ibid., 221.

10. Ibid., 221.

11. "Attack on Black Kettle's Village," 11.

12. *The Civil War in the American West*, 308.

13. Ibid., 309.

14. The biggest problems in investigating this incident were the conflicting stories of participants and the lack of any formal or written record of who said what to whom. It should be noted that there is a time and distance problem associated with these accounts of Chivington's march from Fort Lyon to Sand Creek. If the Sand Creek encampment was actually forty miles away from Fort Lyon and the troops left the Fort at 8:00 p.m., it is highly unlikely they would have covered the distance, on poorly marked trails and in darkness, in less than ten hours. Ten hours of travel would have put them at the Indian village about 6:00 a.m., and give them no more than an hour of remaining darkness in which to encircle the village and prepare for action. Such timing would seem to make it extremely difficult for the men to have had time to lie around drinking whiskey and getting drunk. In truth, it appears that most of what today's histories report on the Sand Creek battle are the result of speculation, rumor, or perjured testimony. Sworn testimony paints a completely different picture. (See Chapter 10.)

–NINE–

Sand Creek

THE SKY WAS BEGINNING TO GET LIGHT in the east, although the sun had not yet appeared over the horizon when Colonel Chivington's troops were finally ready to begin their attack. The soldiers had worked for the better part of an hour to be in position for this moment; the big cannons and the sharpshooters were in place along the crest of several small hills surrounding the village. The firepower could cover every conceivable route of escape. Other soldiers were poised to capture or chase off the Indian ponies tethered at the south side of the village.

As is often the case with "the best laid plans," just as Colonel Chivington was about to give the order to begin firing, a skittish horse bolted, and went racing through the very center of the village. To the surprise of the soldiers, the residents were not still asleep; they were already in places of concealment, waiting for the attack to begin.

The runaway horse was ridden by private George Pierce, Company F, of the First Colorado Volunteers. The panicking animal carried the helpless rider directly in front of a bunker, filled with braves.

Pierce yanked on the bridle. The horse jerked his head to the left and then fell in a heap, tossing private Pierce onto the ground. Pierce leaped to his feet and began running back toward the line of soldiers.

As his friends watched in fascinated, helpless horror, they saw puffs of smoke rise from the Indian rifles. Pierce staggered and stopped, then turned back to face the warriors. There was another series of shots and the soldier dropped dead: the first casualty of the battle of Sand Creek.

There was a split second of silence: an eerie pause that somehow seemed endless. Then there was gunfire

Courtesy Colorado Historical Society

SCENE OF THE OPENING BATTLE
(Looking to the west)

from throughout the village, and from along the hills that surrounded it. The vicious battle that followed lasted for seven hours, and became the focus of a bitter controversy raging for more than 125 years. It was not possible at the time of the battle to find out exactly what transpired, and it certainly is not possible to do so today.

Despite unanimous testimony about the George Pierce incident from officers and men of Colonel Chivington's command, historians today are sharply divided as to whether the troops' presence came as a surprise to the villagers. At least two white traders who lived there, including Julia Bent's husband, Ed Guerrier, testified that the Indians knew the Third Colorado Volunteers had been in the area for several days. What's more, they attested to the tribe's suspicion that the soldiers would come straight to Black Kettle's village. Anticipating of the arrival of the army, they said Chief Black Kettle displayed both an American flag and a white flag of surrender. Hoisted on a pole in front of his tepee the night before the troops arrival, they claimed the flags clearly marked the village as peaceful. According to the traders, the village considered themselves to have surrendered, and under the protection of the army.

Several other modern writers have claimed that Black Kettle hoisted the two flags only after the shooting had started, hoping to stop the gunfire. Those who hold to this later (and currently more popular) version say the presence of the troops came as a complete surprise to the Cheyennes, despite evidence to the contrary.

Many historians ignore the nearly unanimous testimony from the soldiers who participated in the battle. According to these men the Indians, fully prepared for the "surprise" attack, fired the first shots, and no flags of any kind were flying before, during, or after the battle.

Considerable difference of opinion also exists concerning how strongly the village resisted the attack. Colonel Chivington, most of his officers and men maintained that the heavily armed Indians fought back furiously, and never indicated a desire to surrender. To the soldiers, it appeared from the opening shot that this was going to be a fight to the finish—of one side or the other. Both sides said the shooting continued for seven long hours: the length of the battle, alone, indicates that a vicious gun battle was fought at Sand Creek.

However, many of the Indian survivors later claimed that they offered only token resistance, trying on a number of occasions to give themselves up to the soldiers. Most modern accounts of this battle argue that only a relative handful of braves was in the village to begin with, and they tried repeatedly to surrender. They claim that in spite of the spirited resistance, the overwhelming majority of the villagers were elderly men, children, and women who could offer very little in the way of a real battle.

As the shooting started, Captain Luther Wilson, with his troop of 125 men, cut off the Indians from their horses, preventing the braves from mounting them for battle or escape. Soldiers poured deadly howitzer and rifle fire into the center of the village. Warriors raced from burning and collapsing tepees and sought cover behind rocks or in rifle pits which had been carefully prepared in advance. Many women and children fled down the river beds—presumably trying to escape— although even greater numbers apparently joined the men in firing at the soldiers or loading weapons for the warriors.

Sometime well into the fighting, Chief Black Kettle and his wife ran into the stream bed, intending by the chief's own testimony, to join a large group of warriors who were firing back at the soldiers from a rifle pit. As

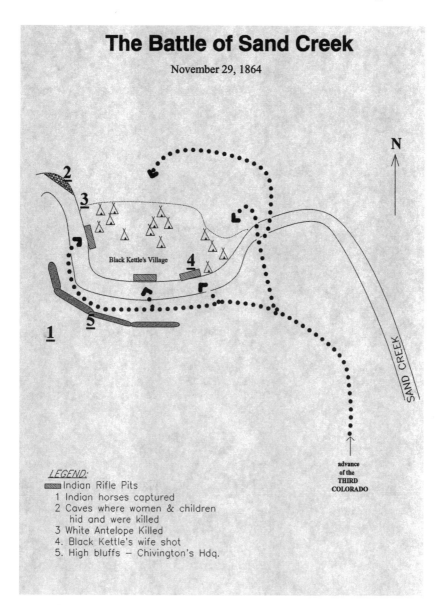

The Battle of Sand Creek

November 29, 1864

N

Black Kettle's Village

SAND CREEK

advance
of the
THIRD
COLORADO

LEGEND:

▨ Indian Rifle Pits

1 Indian horses captured
2 Caves where women & children hid and were killed
3 White Antelope Killed
4. Black Kettle's wife shot
5. High bluffs — Chivington's Hdq.

Courtesy Colorado Historical Society

CAVES IN THE SANDSTONE RIVER BANKS AT SAND CREEK

The bodies of many women and children were found in these caves after the Battle of Sand Creek. Were they "murdered in cold blood by laughing white soldiers," or did they die bearing arms against the white men?

they ran, Black Kettle's wife was hit by gunfire. The woman stumbled but continued running, and was hit again and then again. When at last she fell, Black Kettle thought she was dead; he continued running and soon joined his warriors. Black Kettle later said that his eyes were too bad to do any shooting himself, but that he joined women and children in the pit, reloading rifles and handing them to the younger men who were firing at the soldiers.

Courtesy Colorado Historical Society

YELLOW WOLF

Also known as Yellow Coyote, this was one of the Cheyenne
chiefs who tried to negotiate peace in Denver, but was caught
between his personal desires and the more hostile activities
of younger braves. Yellow Wolf died in the Battle of Sand
Creek.

At the height of the fighting, Chief White Antelope
raced to the top of a small hill and was cut down by
gunfire. One of the enduring stories about the battle of
Sand Creek is that White Antelope was trying
desperately to stop the fighting. Many books claim that
White Antelope shouted repeatedly for the shooting to
stop, trying to tell the soldiers that he had already
surrendered. According to this dramatic legend, when he

could not make himself heard over the din of battle,
White Antelope folded his arms across his chest and
stood waiting to die. The popular legend claims that
while waiting for the fatal bullets, White Antelope was
softly chanting, "nothing lives long except the earth and
mountains."

While this romanticized tale is repeated in nearly
all accounts of the Sand Creek tragedy, logic dictates
that it almost certainly is a figment of someone's
imagination. If the noise of the battle drowned out
White Kettle's shouts, and if he had run to a hill away
from the others as claimed, who could have heard him
softly chanting the death song? Although this picture of
the courageous chief, standing bravely in the midst of
battle waiting to die, seems almost universally accepted,
testimony after the battle indicates White Antelope died
while repeatedly shooting a rifle at the soldiers.

While he was the best known, White Antelope was
not the only chief who died in the fierce battle. At least
eight other chiefs were also killed: among them were
War Bonnet, Left Hand, and Yellow Coyote (who was
also called Yellow Wolf).

Owl Woman was also among the dead. She was the
Cheyenne wife of fur trader William Bent, and the
mother of Mary, Robert, George, Charles, and Julia
Bent. In spite of her death, the elder Bent remained
steadfastly loyal to the Union, fully supporting US Army
action aimed at stopping hostile action on the prairie.
But the killing of Owl Woman seemed to drive George
and Charles into a frenzy of terrorism. During 1865 and
later, the younger Bents were among the most active
and cruel of the hostile Dog Soldiers.

Early in the afternoon, the shooting at Sand Creek
finally began to taper off; by a little after 2:00 PM it
stopped altogether. Many Indians had been killed and

many others had escaped. Still others who had been wounded now lay scattered around the battlefield. For the most part the wounded braves were silent, as one expected from warriors who had always been taught to handle pain and suffering without complaint. But apparently not everything was quiet. Several accounts of the battle say some children—some of them wounded—were crying from various spots around the village. A number of people would later claim that some of the soldiers laughed as they shot and killed the surviving children. One story claims that Colonel Chivington personally killed one or more of the Indian babies. Such stories were denied by virtually everyone present at Sand Creek, but the stories still appear from time to time in written accounts of the tragic battle.

The first reports reaching Colonel Chivington from soldiers who walked through the village after the fighting had stopped was that 500 or more inhabitants had been killed in the hours-long battle; the report was probably greatly exaggerated. Chivington was also told by junior officers that about 500 ponies had been captured, a figure which turned out to be correct. The casualty toll among the soldiers was placed at nine dead and thirty-eight wounded.

Colonel Chivington ordered his troops to search the village. These search parties recovered the fresh scalps of numerous white men and women, although the exact number was never determined. They also recovered bloody clothing of white people, and considerable merchandise that had been taken in attacks on wagon trains and ranches. Except for the human remains, these items were crated up and subsequently returned to Denver for cataloging. Chivington said the scalps, bloody clothing, and booty found in the tepees proved beyond a shadow of a doubt that Indians from this village were hostile and continuing to attack white settlers. Although one would think that the statement is proved by the facts (the physical evidence which was returned to Denver), the claim would be denied over and over again by Chivington's enemies.

Two of the white traders who had been in the village—John S. Smith and Edward Guerrier—were among the battle survivors. Both would later swear that about 500 persons had been in the village when the shooting started, a majority of whom were women and children. Guerrier estimated that only sixty or so braves were among the Cheyennes in the village when the shooting commenced. Guerrier also admitted that the warriors who were in the village fought savagely against the soldiers—testimony that conflicts sharply with later testimony from other sources.

Chief Black Kettle also survived the battle. He, too, said the fighting was fierce. The chief apparently escaped from the village as the shooting was beginning to taper off. Sometime later, after the soldiers left the area, he returned to the battlefield and found his wife in the smoldering remains of the village. To his amazement, she was still alive. Black Kettle picked her up and carried her all the way back to Fort Lyon where he sought medical help for her; she received treatment from the army physicians and survived.

The exact death toll at Sand Creek has never been determined, and remains the subject of considerable debate and wild guesses. The World Book Encyclopedia says, "In 1864, an army force killed nearly 300 peaceful Indians near Sand Creek Colorado. Such events and the revenge they inspired aroused the whole frontier."[1]

Other books claim that up to 500 Native Americans were killed in the attack, which was the casualty number supplied to Colonel Chivington by his own staff.

Almost all of the historical accounts of the battle say that the overwhelming majority of those killed were women and children.

Although repeated testimony at the time placed the death toll somewhere between 300 and 500, there is other evidence that around 130 Indians died at Sand Creek, based on eye-witness claims from survivors and other sources. Of that number, roughly two-thirds were probably women and children. George Bent, who was a notorious liar and hater of the white man—and who therefore had reason to make them look worse than they really were—later gave the toll as being 137 victims. In a letter to Colonel Samuel Tappan, a strong Indian supporter, Bent said that of the 137 who died, only twenty-eight were men of fighting age.[2]

In trying to cull the truth from all the claims pertaining to Sand Creek, it should be remembered that each side had considerably more at stake than the battle itself. George Bent, a star witness against Colonel Chivington, was an ex–Confederate soldier and a Cheyenne Dog Soldier. He had participated in numerous documented attacks against whites, and hated them intensely. As a Confederate, he may have hated John Chivington because of Chivington's Civil War record; Chivington was usually credited (or blamed, depending on one's point of view) for the crushing defeat of the Confederates' Western Expeditionary Force in New Mexico two years earlier.

Some sources suggest that both George and Charles Bent were among the Confederate agents who were actively recruiting, arming, and training hostile Indians in Colorado, but no hard evidence exists to support such a theory.

As a Dog Soldier, George Bent hated Chivington because he was the commander of soldiers responsible for finding and stopping the Dog Soldiers. Bent's mother was killed at Sand Creek—another adequate reason for his hatred of the white man in general, and Colonel Chivington in particular. And although most other accounts of the battle ignore it, the truth is that Bent himself was painfully wounded at Sand Creek—shot in the hip. He did fully recover within a few weeks,[3] although his hatred for Chivington was unquestionably intensified by this painful injury.

Colonel Samuel Tappan later testified that the battle at Sand Creek was nothing more than a slaughter of Indian innocents, but Tappan may also have had special motives in attacking the soldiers involved in the battle. At the time the troops of the First Colorado Volunteers unanimously voted to make John Chivington. their commander in the Civil War battle of Glorieta Pass, Samuel Tappan was already a full colonel in the outfit in which Chivington was a mere major. It seems at least possible that Tappan was upset over the troops' selection of the more junior Chivington rather than Tappan himself to be their leader. Although Tappan testified about the massacre at Sand Creek, he was not present when the battle was fought, and there is no evidence he ever visited the battlefield afterwards.

When the shooting finally ended that afternoon, the soldiers hung around the battle site for the remainder of the day, tending to their wounded, burying dead, and otherwise going through the normal post-battle routine. They reveled in what they believed had been a great and hard-fought victory.

The following morning, Chivington ordered his troops back to Denver for rest and relaxation. Along the way, Chivington stopped and sent telegrams to Governor Evans (and possibly also to newspaper publisher Bill Byers). Chivington said that the Third Colorado had acquitted itself well by wiping out a huge camp of hostile Indians, probably including the hated Cheyenne Dog Soldier Chief Roman Nose. He repeated that "perhaps 500 of the hostiles" were killed.

The resulting *Rocky Mountain News* stories touched off great rejoicing among the people of Colorado; it seemed that white men had finally taken some revenge for the hundreds of settlers, pioneers, ranchers, traders, and fur trappers killed in Indian attacks over the past year. The front page screamed:

GREAT BATTLE WITH INDIANS!
THE SAVAGES DISPERSED!
500 INDIANS KILLED
OUR LOSS 9 KILLED, 38 WOUNDED

The lengthy newspaper article quoted Colonel Chivington as saying, "I, at daylight this morning, attacked a Cheyenne village of 130 lodges, from 900 to 1,000 warriors strong. We killed Chiefs Black Kettle, White Antelope, and Little Robe, and between four and five hundred others."

The paper also carried an eyewitness report from one of the soldiers, who said that the men of the Third Colorado had, "gained the greatest victory west of the Missouri, over the savages. We have completely broken up the tribe and think the settlers will not be further molested by them."[4] The newspaper reported that Roman Nose "likely" was among the many braves killed in the fighting.

Interestingly, the third page of the newspaper report quoted trappers John Smith and Ed Guerrier as saying there were no more than 100 lodges with a total of no more than 500 persons in the Cheyenne village. The two traders were quoted as saying, "two thirds of the people in the village were women and children," and "the adults in the camp were mostly women." Few people at the time appeared to take note of the conflicting information from the traders.

The citizens of Denver, and the entire West, were elated at the news—especially the news that Roman Nose was probably among the dead. On December 12, the men of the Third Colorado were formally honored with a parade through the streets of downtown Denver. They were roundly praised by virtually everyone in the city and the mood throughout the Territory was one of almost giddy celebration.

Then the other boot dropped. Within seventy-two hours after the return of the soldiers to Denver questions began to surface about the Third Colorado's great victory. The first hint of trouble actually came in the form of a note hidden deep in Colonel Chivington's official report to General Curtis. The note severely chastised one of Chivington's most veteran officers for refusing to participate in the battle and for failing to fire a single shot. The tell-tale paragraph was the final item in Chivington's formal report on Sand Creek:

> I cannot conclude this report without saying that the conduct of Captain Silas S. Soule, Company D, First Cavalry of Colorado, was at least ill-advised, he saying that he thanked God that he had killed no Indians and like expressions. Under the circumstances, I am considering whether to file formal charges against this officer.[5]

The accusation against Captain Soule, had anyone taken notice, should have been strong evidence that something was terribly wrong. Silas Soule had fought alongside Chivington in the Civil War battles at (and subsequent to) Glorieta Pass. He was one of Chivington's most trusted officers as well as being a personal friend. He was a decorated war hero who had demonstrated that he was not afraid to fight.

The tragic story of Captain Soule is an intriguing part of the Sand Creek story. Soule had objected to the attack against Black Kettle's village, possibly as soon as the attack was planned and certainly well before the shooting started. Soule later told friends that as he looked over the Cheyenne village he came to the realization that the village contained mostly women and children. For that reason, he said, he pleaded with Chivington to halt the attack. Soule said Chivington became angry and ordered Soule back to his post.

Afterward, when the troops returned to Denver, Soule and several other men told anyone who would listen that the battle was not as it was portrayed in the *Rocky Mountain News*. In fact, they said that Cheyenne women and children were cruelly and deliberately massacred in the battle, and that old men were killed as they waved flags of surrender. They were quoted as saying that they saw drunken soldiers laughing as they shot helpless, cowering, unarmed and non–hostile Indians.

These accusations—now considered among the most damning to Colonel Chivington—were not believed at first. In fact, they were deeply resented by people who had finally been given the victory for which they had longed since even before the brutal Hungate murders. Soon the people of Denver were openly criticizing Captain Soule and the others who were speaking out against Colonel Chivington, saying that these men were cowards who had no right to be called soldiers.

Courtesy Colorado Historical Society

CAPTAIN SILAS SOULE

Although a hero of the Civil War, he refused to participate in the Sand Creek fighting. Court-martialed by Colonel Chivington, Soule became the center of the controversy over the actions of the Third Colorado. He was bushwhacked while awaiting a chance to tell his side of the story.

Three days after returning from Sand Creek, Colonel Chivington filed a series of formal charges against Captain Soule and five other men who had refused to participate in the battle. The charges against the captain said that Soule was, "a coward and a deserter in time of battle, [an officer] who abandoned his leadership post, disobeyed lawful orders of his superiors, refused to fight when the battle got underway, and—in fact—threw down his weapon and ran from the scene of the battle."[6]

Chivington ordered the six accused men placed under arrest pending a court martial. The charges were most serious, and because there was no military brig at Camp Weld near Denver, the accused men were incarcerated at the Denver City jail.

Captain Soule's wife was one of the few persons who believed in him; she began writing regularly to Secretary of War Stanton and others in Washington, pleading for her husband's release from jail. As the controversy over Sand Creek began to escalate, both the army and the U. S. Congress started talking about a formal investigation of Sand Creek.

Friday, December 23. Secretary Stanton telegraphed Governor Evans, ordering that Captain Soule and the other accused men be released from jail on personal recognizance bonds pending the outcome of a formal military inquiry into all events surrounding Sand Creek. It was anticipated that Captain Soule would be one of the leading witnesses in that planned investigation.

Wednesday, December 28. Silas Soule was walking along a downtown Denver street when he was bushwhacked by a gunman who apparently was hiding in an alley. The bullet struck Soule in the middle of the back and killed him outright. His murder was never solved.

Well before Soule was killed, even before he released from jail, it became apparent to many people that something seemed terribly wrong with the battle at Sand Creek. Indians and friends of Indians, including the fur trappers and the six soldiers already mentioned, were saying that Sand Creek was not a glorious victory for the soldiers. It was, they charged, a cold-blooded massacre of mostly unarmed and friendly Indians who had surrendered at Fort Lyon and considered themselves to be under the protection of the army that attacked them.

Several other soldiers now wrote letters to various army and government officials, accusing the men who participated in the attack of having committed "awful depredations." Some charged that well before the attack started it was known to army officers and men that the occupants of the Cheyenne village believed they had surrendered to and were under the protection of the US Army. Most, if not all, of the accusatory letters did not come from soldiers who participated in the battle, but rather from US Army regulars who remained behind at Fort Lyon. It would be some time before evidence was offered to explain this sudden outpouring of letters from soldiers who had stayed at Fort Lyon during the battle.

Within a period of weeks the entire nation was caught up in the controversy raging over Sand Creek. The Time–Life book on American Indians says Eastern newspapers began publishing the letters, and soon there was a congressional outcry against Colonel Chivington and his men. The book says that Ulysses S. Grant wrote to Governor Evans, saying that Sand Creek was nothing more or less than a murder carried out by Federal troops, of people who thought they were under army protection. If such a letter were actually written, it apparently was based solely on newspaper stories, letters and hearsay; Grant did not visit Colorado before or after the tragedy, nor is there any evidence he talked to anyone involved. But as the investigation continued, the army's Judge Advocate–General, Joseph Holt, said publicly that the battle at Sand Creek was, "a cowardly and cold-blooded slaughter, sufficient to cover its perpetrators with indelible infamy, and the face of every American with shame and indignation."[7]

Colonel Chivington and most of the men under his command cried foul, and repeatedly swore that the battle had been exactly as they described it, not as their enemies now portrayed it. By now the situation was completely out of hand; the US Congress ordered one full-scale investigation and the army ordered another. Eastern newspapers were filled with mostly guess-work articles on the "outrage" at Sand Creek. And in time, most of the world seemed united in condemning John Chivington and the Third Colorado Volunteers for what they supposed transpired at Sand Creek.

Notes

1. *World Book Encyclopedia* (World Book, Inc., Chicago, 1983) Book W–X–Y–Z, 195.
2. David Berthrong, *The Southern Cheyennes* (University of Oklahoma Press, 1975) 219–20.
3. Ruth Dunn, "Attack on Black Kettle's Village and the Prelude to Sand Creek" Unpublished Notes, Heritage Collection, Lincoln, Nebraska Public Library, 4–8.
4. *The Indians* (Time–Life Books, New York, 1973), 183.
5. Ibid., 183.
6. Ibid., 186.
7. Ibid., 187.

–TEN–

The Accusers

THE FORMAL INVESTIGATIONS of the Sand Creek incident were conducted in a manner that raise many legal and ethical questions. Although today the conclusions are generally considered to be correct, an actual court of law would choke on the procedures employed and the unsupported statements (from both sides) admitted into evidence.

The US Senate investigation, spearheaded by an old foe of American Indian policy, Senator James Doolittle, was conducted primarily at Bent's Fort, although some testimony was taken at both Fort Lyon and Denver. The witnesses invited to testify included virtually all of Chivington's enemies, as well as enemies of the policies he enforced. Two dozen of the most militant Cheyennes—including George and Charles Bent—were invited to testify. A dozen other fur traders who lived among the Cheyennes, including such names as Guerrier, Beckwourth, and Smith were summoned as witnesses. Kit Carson and William Bent were called as "expert" witnesses, with no reference to Carson's responsibility for the deaths of three to five thousand

Navajos two years earlier. The list of witnesses is notable for its almost total lack of defense witnesses— those who might testify on behalf of John Chivington and the Third Colorado.

The senate's witnesses were virtually unanimous in charging that there were almost no males in Black Kettle's village, that the men who were there were either very old or very young, that all of them considered themselves to have surrendered to the army, that these were obviously peaceful Indians who sought no trouble with whites, and that John Chivington knew the Indians had surrendered. Additionally, they charged that the Indians at Sand Creek flew flags of surrender, offered little resistance to the military and were incapable of offering much resistance; that Chivington encouraged or participated in atrocities (including rape and the calculated murder of Indian babies) and that the attack was really a part of Chivington's planned political campaign for the US Congress.

By comparison to the senate hearings, the army's investigation, conducted in Denver, seemed considerably more balanced. Although many of the senate's witnesses were invited to speak, so were a number of persons defending Chivington. Even then, nearly three times as many witnesses opposed to the military action were called as those supporting the Sand Creek attack (even though the general population and the men of Chivington's command appeared to have overwhelmingly supported both Chivington and the army's action).

In both formal investigations, there were numerous charges—including testimony about John Chivington's purported thinking and personal motives—without any evidence to support the accusations. Much of the testimony against Chivington and the Third Colorado was clearly perjurious, and would not have been

Courtesy Colorado Historical Society

KIT CARSON, FRONTIER SCOUT

Senate investigators called him to testify as an expert witness to prove that Chivington mishandled Indians. They—and history—seem to have forgotten that Carson was responsible for the freezing and starvation deaths of 4,000 Navajos committed to his care in New Mexico.

accepted in any court. A great deal of the testimony at the military hearings was obviously designed to distance the army's highest ranking officers from Sand Creek. They sought to show that the Third Colorado went far beyond orders in attacking and destroying Black Kettle's village.

Colonel Chivington's political enemies in Colorado—those who opposed statehood and those who considered running against him for Congress included— added their voices to the clamor against him. They had a field day with the rumors and suggestions that Sand Creek was something other than what it appeared to be. Suddenly it seemed that there were Chivington critics everywhere.

Among the most vocal of these Chivington enemies was the United States District Attorney for Colorado, Sam E. Browne. The liberal Browne and the conservative Chivington were long time political foes, having clashed both publicly and privately on virtually every issue facing the territory.

Not asked to testify at either hearing, Browne nonetheless took advantage of the opportunity to speak out frequently against Chivington. Browne claimed that he had once heard the colonel say that he wanted to take no prisoners from among the Indians, and that he planned to "kill and scalp all, little and big."[1] In spite of the well-known and long-standing hostility between Browne and Chivington, no subsequent investigators of the incident seem to question whether Browne actually heard Chivington make such a statement—even though Chivington steadfastly swore he never said any such thing.

Eastern newspapers and many of Chivington's Colorado critics also now claimed that the colonel had said that the only good Indian is a dead Indian. None of the reports specified exactly where or when such a statement was made, yet it was widely quoted and believed by the Eastern press. Although it is possible Chivington made such a statement, other history records credit the famous comment to General Philip H. Sheridan, during an argument with a Comanche leader.[2]

Attorney General Browne, however, was not the only leader of the anti–Chivington attack; Lieutenant John Cramer joined in the criticism. Cramer claimed he and Chivington got into a heated argument at Fort Lyon just before the troops began their march on Sand Creek. The issue, says Cramer, was whether the Indians camped on the creek had surrendered and considered themselves at peace with and under the protection of the US Army. Cramer told military investigators that Chivington dismissed his concerns, saying that under the orders issued by General Curtis, no Indians met the criteria for surrender and that all Indians, therefore, were considered to be at war with the United States. Although it was clear that those were, indeed, the frequently repeated orders from Chivington's commander, critics now said that Chivington should have disobeyed such orders.

Lieutenant Cramer also claimed that he heard Chivington say, "Damn any man who sympathizes with the Indians."[3] In 1864, the word damn was extremely foul language. Most people in Colorado discounted the claim at the time, since Chivington—a preacher, elder, and national leader of the most conservative faction of his denomination—did not use profanity. However, the Cramer quotation, picked up by Eastern newspapers, soon became part of the enduring legend which many now accept as the simple and unquestioned truth about John Chivington. It helped to solidify public opinion against Chivington and the alleged actions of his soldiers at Sand Creek.

Soon, claims filed by other men—some of whom were at Sand Creek and many of whom were not— became a part of the mounting so-called hard evidence against Chivington. Lieutenant Cramer began remembering more and more damaging information about Chivington. Several days after his initial testimony, Cramer added that the colonel had also told some of his officers that he "had come to kill all [the Indians], and believed it to be honorable to kill Indians under any and all circumstances."[4]

There is considerable evidence that John Chivington (like most other whites in the West) had concluded that there was no way to deal peacefully with the Indians. Several times the *Rocky Mountain News* quoted him as saying that because of the demonstrated hostility of the Indians, the only hope for settlers was in the killing of all Indians in the territory. This certainly was not a unique stance. Probably most frontiersmen (and women) believed that Indians were unreliable and murderous, and should be wiped out. One modern history says:

> Caught up in their own problems, the thousands of settlers were unable to judge the Indians in any but Anglo-American terms. The decade of war was the result not merely of competition for needed land, but also of the friction between two dissimilar cultures.

According to the same writers, when the Senate investigators showed up in Denver, citizens of the community lined the street and "screamed at senators holding hearings on the Indian problem the single phrase: 'Exterminate them! Exterminate them!'"[5]

As the press carried daily accusations against the Third Colorado the outcry against Chivington became like a boulder careening down a Colorado mountainside; there was no way to stop it. The motive for such accusations was questioned by most Coloradans at the time, but author David Lavender is one of the few modern historians who recognize that at least some of the anti–Chivington criticism may have been pure politics. Lavender says, "Always his [political] opponents in Colorado would accuse him of deliberately stirring up Indian battles in order to make a reputation and attract votes."[6]

As the days passed, an increasingly long list of people lined up to testify against the tarnished Colorado hero. Included in that list were a number of fur traders. Eastern newspapers at the time pointed out that since this damaging information came from other white men, it almost certainly was true—and many historians still accept that.

In truth, the testimony of the traders should be weighed in view of what is actually known about the men. First, and most obvious, is that fur traders stood to gain considerable stature among the tribes—and be in a position to earn considerably more money from them—by lining up on the Indian side of the issue. That does not necessarily mean that the traders were dishonest, or that they necessarily had an ulterior motive for their anti–Chivington testimony or what they said was untrue—but it certainly should raise some flags of caution.

The second item of consideration is that three of the fur traders who spoke against Chivington were married to Cheyenne women at the time. All of them counted on trade with Cheyennes for their very existence. Several were living in Black Kettle's village at the time of the attack. Some were known liars and thieves—and worse.

Although the people of Colorado remained for the most part solidly behind Colonel Chivington and the Third Colorado Volunteers, clearly the rest of the world lined up solidly against them. Chivington appeared genuinely baffled by the sudden outcries in Congress, the Department of War and the Eastern press—all of them condemning him in public before even talking to him in private.

By late December the first formal investigation into what was now called the Sand Creek Massacre began in Denver; at least two more formal investigations would follow over the next eighteen months. As the territory began its probe of the incident, the US Congress authorized its own investigation, and the army announced it would consider whether to look into the matter. Ironically, the congressional probe was delayed since congressmen were unable to travel to Denver by conventional methods; Indian raids had closed all the roads from Kansas City to Denver. Deeming it necessary to take testimony from numerous people in Colorado, the on-site congressional investigation delayed several months until the Washington delegation could reach Denver by sailing around South America, landing in California and then traveling eastward through Arizona and northward through New Mexico.

Shortly after the first of the near year, Colonel Chivington complained to the *Rocky Mountain News:*

> I am not being treated fairly. My record is well known, well documented. So is the record of the Indians. It isn't me who killed the Hungates. It isn't me who shut down the roads from Kansas City. I am not the reason the mines are closed and the Territory is starving. Yet

it suddenly is a crime for a man to defend himself and his country.[7]

In February, just a little over two months after the Sand Creek Massacre, an obviously frustrated Chivington was quoted in the same newspaper as saying, "Damn anyone who sympathizes with the Indians. I came to kill Indians and I believe it was right to use any means under God's heaven to accomplish that task. I stand by Sand Creek!"[8] (There wass that swear word again.)

Wednesday, January 11, 1865. Army chief of staff, General Henry Halleck, sent a telegram to General Samuel Curtis at Fort Leavenworth, Kansas. In part, Halleck's wire said:

> Statements from respectable sources have been received here that the conduct of Colonel Chivington's command towards the friendly Indians have been a series of outrages calculated to make them all hostile. You will inquire into and report on this matter.[9]

By the time those three separate investigations were underway, the press had clearly concluded that Colonel Chivington was a butcher who deliberately attacked and destroyed a peaceful village. The Eastern newspapers portrayed him as a man who enjoyed killing little children. Several newspapers carried the astonishing accusation that Chivington was in the Cheyenne village "bashing out the brains" of babies. Another favorite charge of the newspapers was that Chivington had brought three Indian babies back to Denver and sold them to a carnival, from which government agents rescued them. Apparently, only the newspapers took such accusations seriously.

When the formal military investigation of Sand
Creek opened in Denver, one of the first witnesses called
was fur trader Jim Beckwourth. His testimony was
lengthy and extremely detailed; it was one of the most
damaging against Chivington. Beckwourth said that he
personally heard Chivington speaking as his troops
prepared to open fire at Sand Creek, "Men, strip for
action. I don't tell you to kill all ages and sexes, but look
back on the plains of the Platte, where your mothers,
fathers, brothers and sisters have been slain, their blood
saturating the sands of the Platte."[10] If Beckwourth
really gave that verbatim testimony as widely reported,
it must have been composed for him by someone else.
Beckwourth's own speech was the coarse language an
uneducated, illiterate frontiersman; he was not likely to
have talked on his own about "blood saturating the
sands of the Platte."

Defense witnesses would later point out that
Beckwourth could not have heard such an order from
Chivington, since Beckwourth was not even present at
the battle. Reliable testimony from many other sources
(including the personal testimony of Robert Bent who
had guided the troops to Black Kettle's village) said that
Beckwourth did leave Fort Lyon with the troops the
night before the battle. However, Bent and others said
that Beckwourth became ill a short time later and asked
to return to the fort.[11] Yet Beckwourth testified in great
detail about the individual and collective acts of atrocity
he swore he personally witnessed being committed by
Colonel Chivington's troops during the attack.

Because Jim Beckwourth's testimony was so
damaging, and is still widely quoted as proof of the
charges against Chivington, it is important to take a
closer look at the life of this man.

Courtesy Colorado Historical Society

JIM BECKWOURTH, "THE GAUDY LIAR"

Beckwourth was the key prosecution witness against John Chivington and the Third Colorado, and his testimony is still widely believed. However, Beckwourth was really a cold-blooded murderer, horse thief, armed robber, con man, bigamist, and liar. Sworn affidavits say he made up his testimony against Chivington in order to bilk the government out of thousands of dollars.

Beckwourth first came to the attention of territorial officials in 1835, when he was accused of illegally selling whiskey to Indians. When confronted, Beckwourth not only admitted doing so, he bragged about it, pointing out that he could buy whiskey by the keg in St. Louis for twenty-five cents a gallon. He would then add four gallons of water to each gallon of whiskey, producing five gallons of fire water. Each pint of this watered-down mixture was swapped for five to eight dollars worth of buffalo robes and other goods. Those same goods, returned to St. Louis, could be sold for five to six times what the traders paid for them in Colorado. Thus to trader Beckwourth, twenty-five cents worth of whiskey frequently returned a profit of $800 or more.

Beckwourth once wrote to friends about this short-cut to wealth (the wording is paraphrased):

> Let the reader sit down and figure up the profits on a forty gallon cask of alcohol and he will be thunder struck, or rather, whiskey struck. When disposed of, four gallons of water are added to each gallon of whiskey. In 200 gallons there are 1600 pints, for each one of which the trader gets a buffalo robe worth five dollars.[12]

Beckwourth was the son of a white man named Beckwith and a black slave woman; why or when he changed his name to Beckwourth is not clear. Around 1850, a ghost writer visited Beckwourth and wrote a highly fanciful biography that earned for Beckwourth the nickname The Gaudy Liar—a name by which he was known throughout the frontier for the rest of his life.

Among the stories which Beckwourth swore were true was one in which an entire tribe of attacking Blackfeet Indians chased him, on foot, in southern Wyoming. Beckwourth said he not only eluded "100 attacking injuns," but says he did so by running ninety-five miles in a single day.

Beckwourth claimed that the Crows adopted him, when he was already a grown man and a fur trader. They eventually made him chief of the tribe, in recognition of his bravery and leadership. Later, Beckwourth says he led his Crow warriors in a battle against the Blackfeet, "I advanced directly upon their lines and had struck down my man before the others came up...seeing me engage hand to hand with the enemy's whole force [the remainder of the Crows] immediately came to my assistance. Now I was the greatest of their party."[13]

As Beckwourth's reputation as a liar grew, most of his fellow fur trappers began to shun him. Sometimes there was more to it than simply disbelieving him; another trapper named Thomas Fitzpatrick once filed formal charges against Beckwourth. Fitzpatrick accused Beckwourth of robbing him at gun point; eventually, the charges were dismissed because there were no witnesses.

Beckwourth claimed he enlisted in the US Army under an alias, and fought under the command of Zachary Taylor during the Seminole Wars in Florida in 1837. The claim was never verified.

In 1839, Beckwourth was with—he says he led—a group of Utes who tried to steal a huge herd of 5,000 horses from Spanish explorers in California's Santa Ana Valley. Records indicate that Beckwourth really did show up at Bent's fort late in 1839 with a huge herd of horses that he traded to local Indians. Flushed with success, Beckwourth says he made three additional horse-stealing trips to California, each being more successful than the one preceding it. That confession by

Beckwourth, of course, made him a horse thief—the lowest form of humanity on the frontier.

The *Encyclopedia of American Crime*[14] says that Beckwourth was the organizer and head of "the greatest gang of horse thieves in California history." The book also says Beckwourth had murdered a number of lawmen and civilians in a series of bar room brawls and bush-whackings throughout the West.

Beckwourth and several other traders eventually established their own trading post. The post was quite successful and eventually grew to become the city of Pueblo, Colorado.

Beckwourth was married numerous times, often to several women simultaneously. He usually married the daughter of a local chief or Mexican trader with whom Beckwourth did business. None of his marriages lasted for any length of time, although few were ever formally dissolved.

In February of 1845, Beckwourth joined the Spanish rebel army of Jose Castro, and apparently participated in the Battle of Cahuenga Pass, California. He quit the rebel army right after the battle and by his own admission, stole numerous horses from the army and headed back to Colorado to trade them.

Beckwourth eventually went south and settled at Santa Fe, New Mexico. When the Mexican–American war erupted, Beckwourth claimed he was asked to join the US Army as a courier (which may be true); Beckwourth says that in that role he became a military hero. He claimed to have fought with the US when the Americans overwhelmed the Mexicans at Taos; records do not confirm any of those claims.

In 1861, Beckwourth took another new Indian bride, moved to Denver, and became a store keeper. A few months later he was divorced and working as a barber in the same town. Two months later he was a farmer with another new Indian bride, working just outside Denver.

Records indicate he enlisted as an army scout for future Colorado governor E. L. Berthoud in 1862. While serving in that post he was accused of stealing from the army and was given a bad-conduct discharge from the service. At about the same time, he killed another man in a barroom brawl, but the fight was ruled self defense and no charges were filed.

In the early fall of 1862, Governor Evans hired fur traders to visit all the tribes in eastern Colorado, asking their chiefs to attend treaty talks at Bent's Fort. The tribes sent back word that they were too busy hunting to attend the conference. Weeks later, Evans tried again, and again the chiefs refused to come. Evans was baffled by this refusal until several sources told him that the fur traders, serving as his messengers, personally opposed the conference. These reports said the traders actively discouraged Indians from attending peace talks because any new treaty might restrict the traders' access to furs, from which they made their living. Evans later told associates that the fur traders involved in the treachery were Joseph Bissonette, Jim Beckwourth, John and Jack Smith, and Ed Guerrier.[15] Three of the five would later testify against John Chivington, and a fourth was killed at Sand Creek.

In 1863, Beckwourth was back to trading with Indians. As usual, he married a Cheyenne squaw and moved in with Black Kettle's village to improve his standing with the tribe. He was still living with the tribe, but was not in the village at the time of the Sand Creek battle.

This, then, is the man whose testimony was considered the most vital—and, along with George Bent,

most believable—in the case against Colonel John
Chivington. It was the testimony of a liar, killer, horse
thief, bigamist, and an opportunist, drummed out of the
service with a bad conduct discharge. For some reason,
none of this history of Jim Beckwourth ever appears in
modern historical accounts of the battle at Sand Creek.

Testimony from others may have been equally
tainted. Another key witness against John Chivington
was fur trapper John Smith, who told investigators that
Chivington had personally ordered and possibly
participated in the wanton killing of Indian women and
children. Had anyone checked, they would have
discovered some interesting facts about Smith that
made his testimony also highly suspect.

Smith's wife was a Cheyenne woman. His son, Jack
Smith, died during the Sand Creek fighting. John Smith
claimed that Chivington personally ordered the
execution of the younger Smith after his capture. Author
David Lavender says that at the time of Sand Creek,
John Smith, "was said to be making a fortune helping
Indian Agent Colley and Colley's son cheat the Indians
out of their annuities."[16]

There is a great deal more to the story than simple
dishonesty. Like most other information about Sand
Creek, there is great confusion and inaccuracy in
modern literature on the subject of the Smiths, father
and son. Paul Wellman claims that Colonel Chivington
kidnapped Jack Smith at Fort Lyon, and forced Smith to
guide the Third Colorado to Black Kettle's village.
Wellman suggests that the soldiers murdered Jack
shortly after he arrived at the village.[17]

Soldiers, involved in the battle at Sand Creek,
apparently did shoot Jack Smith, and there is little
question that his death lay heavily on John Chivington.
According to testimony at the army's hearings, Jack

Smith's capture occurred at about the mid point of the battle. One of the soldiers asked John Chivington what to do with him. Soldiers testified that Chivington refused to intervene on Smith's behalf, so the soldiers took Smith to a nearby hill and shot him.

While that apparently truthful report may horrify people, there is additional information that may help explain both Chivington's seeming indifference and the soldiers' cruelty. First, consider the mood of the citizens of Colorado; in a state of siege, the isolated territory was facing starvation because of Indian attacks. Hundreds of people were raped, tortured, kidnapped, and killed in the past few months. General Curtis had given John Chivington specific and repeated orders to punish those responsible for atrocities against whites.

The younger Smith personally and actively participated in a number of gruesome attacks. Both Indians and whites accused him in the kidnapping, torture, rape, and eventual trading of a white woman, while in southern Colorado a few months before Sand Creek.

Bent's Fort tells that Jack Smith was with a band of Cheyennes who wiped out a three-wagon government supply train in July of 1864. Among the travelers with the wagon train was a family of four persons. According to the book:

> Before the mother's eyes the husband was "mutilated in a way shocking to relate" and the children were brained [heads smashed in]. Jack [Smith] then passed the woman on the prairie to his followers. Unfortunately surviving this, the next night she managed to hang herself from a lodgepole.[18]

According to testimony at the army investigation of Sand Creek, Jack Smith was captured alive by

Lieutenant Clark Dunn and several enlisted men. Dunn said that at the height of the fighting he took Smith to Chivington and asked what to do with Smith. Dunn claims that Chivington shouted over the din of the battle, "Don't ask me; you know my orders. I want no prisoners."[19] Dunn says that the troops led Smith a short distance away and killed him revenge for the murder and rape of the white family. Whatever the contributing factors, Smith's execution produced some of the most damaging testimony as to the character and mind-set of Colonel Chivington at the time of the battle.

Other facts about Sand Creek are not so simple or straight-forward as they first appeared to be. For example, many persons who have written about Sand Creek seem to miss the point when they comment on the presence of fur trader Ed Guerrier in Black Kettle's village. Some have said that Guerrier was a friend of whites and his mere presence in the village was "pretty good proof in itself that the Indians were peaceful."[20] This seems typical of misinformation and erroneous conclusions about Sand Creek. In truth, Guerrier was in the village because he was married to Julia Bent, a member of Black Kettle's tribe and the daughter of Owl Woman, another member of the tribe. In addition, frontier fur traders nearly always lived among the Indians because it made their work so much simpler.

Probably the most graphic and most compelling testimony about atrocities committed by the soldiers at Sand Creek came from Chivington's reluctant guide, Robert Bent. Keep in mind that Bent himself led the troops to Black Kettle's village, that Bent's mother died in the attack, and one of his brothers was wounded. That, of course, does not make his anti–Chivington testimony untrue, but it may cast it in a somewhat different light. Bent told investigators that in the course of the battle:

> I saw five squaws hiding under a bank. When troops came up to them they ran out and showed their persons to let the soldiers know that they were squaws. They begged for mercy, but the soldiers shot them all. I saw on squaw lying on a bank, whose leg had been broken by a shell. A soldier came up to her with a drawn saber. She raised her arm to protect herself when he struck, breaking her arm; she rolled over and raised the other arm when he struck again, breaking it. Then he left without killing her.
>
> Some thirty or forty squaws and children collected in a hole for protection. [They] sent out a little girl about six years old with a white flag on a stick. She was shot and killed and all the [others] in the hole were killed.
>
> I saw one squaw cut open with an unborn child lying by her side. I saw the body of White Antelope with his privates cut off, and I heard a soldier say he was going to make a tobacco pouch out of them. I saw one squaw whose privates had been cut out. I saw a little girl who had been hid in the sand. Two soldiers drew their pistols and shot her, then pulled her out of the sand by the arm. I saw quite a number of infants in arms killed along with their mothers.[21]

There was equally distressing testimony from several other witnesses who said that some soldiers scalped the Indians, including some wounded who were not yet dead. There is a question whether wounded warriors were scalped, but little doubt that soldiers scalped those who were dead. White soldiers now commonly scalped their Indian victims, just as Indians routinely scalped the whites. The army appears to have made little effort to discourage such tactics on the western frontier, although General Henry Sibley felt revulsion when he learned his soldiers had done so during the 1862 Minnesota uprising by Santee Sioux.

Just because it was a common practice on the plains
does not make it right, but it does make its toleration
more understandable.

Several people testified that some soldiers
mutilated the warriors' bodies, and such testimony is
almost certainly accurate. This sort of uncivilized
barbarity was also not unusual at the time; it occurred
in the wake of many battles. Routinely, braves mutilated
the bodies of their victims. Again, just because it was
common practice does not make it right—but it was
common, and had considerable precedence before Sand
Creek—and continued for a dozen years afterward.

Much of the sworn testimony against Chivington
revolved around what he allegedly told his troops at
Fort Lyon just before they left for Sand Creek. A number
of soldiers testified that they specifically heard
Chivington say to his troops something on the order of
the following:

> I want to make it clear that we are in an all-out war.
> It is a war that is to be waged at its fullest. The enemy
> has granted no quarter and must be given no quarter.
> I am not interested in prisoners. I am not interested in
> seeing Indians surrender or promise to be peaceful in
> the future. The Indian cannot be trusted. He is a liar
> and a thief. Besides, we are not equipped to handle
> prisoners; we have no facilities for them. Our job is to
> eradicate the vermin infesting the Great Plains and to
> make this a safe place to live. The only way to do that
> is to wage total war, without mercy. The ranchers and
> farmers, the businessmen, the mothers and fathers
> and children of Colorado are counting on us. We must
> be quick and we must be thorough. The Indian menace
> must be completely eradicated.

Chivington repeatedly denied making any of those
statements on the eve of Sand Creek, although he

admitted making some similar comments when speaking to public gatherings in Denver several weeks before the battle. Chivington also said over and over that his intent was to kill only those Indians who had murdered whites.

Another accusation made by several soldiers was that, when asked what to do with Indian women and children, Chivington responded:

> We are under specific orders; we are to take no prisoners. We are to punish the Indians. As for their women and children, "nits make lice," as they say. A surviving squaw will have babies who grow up to be even more bloodthirsty braves, whom our children would have to deal with. Our orders are clear. There is to be no future generation of Roman Noses harassing white men.

The "nits make lice" quotation is the one most often cited as evidence that Chivington deliberately sought to kill women and children. Chivington apparently really did make such a statement, but it came as he spoke to a political rally in Denver two months before Sand Creek—not at Fort Lyon on the eve of the battle, or at the height of the fighting, itself.

Those opposing Colonel Chivington claimed that troops under his command had frequently, on earlier occasions, been too aggressive in pursuing Indians. Specifically, these sources mentioned Lieutenant Eayre's confrontation and those of Lieutenant Dunn months before Sand Creek. The critics said that it was common knowledge that the soldiers attacked the Indians, and that Indians had verified those charges.

Eastern newspapers reported each of these accusations with apparent glee, giving them prominence in the press. Virtually nowhere did anyone defend

Chivington and the Third Colorado. Letters to the editor of New York and other Eastern newspapers were angry and virtually unanimous in their outrage and condemnation of Chivington's command.

In Congress, numerous lawmakers spoke unanimously in presuming the guilt of Chivington and the soldiers. The Bureau of Indian Affairs said the attacks reflected the type of barbaric thinking practiced by the army, and made peace impossible. The army sought to distance itself from Chivington, suggesting that his actions were unauthorized and probably illegal, and that they planned a full-scale investigation of the charges in the near future.

Only on the western frontier did Chivington continue to enjoy popular support. Most citizens of the West, and especially those of Colorado, stood by Chivington and the actions of his troops. As the pressure mounted, it became more and more politically unwise for leaders of the Republican party to continue to identify with Chivington. After all, Colorado could not gain statehood without an act of Congress—and Congress was not likely to authorize statehood knowing that the man most likely to run for (and possibly be elected) to Congress was this so-called butcher they were so busy denouncing. Governor Evans, Bill Byers, and other conservative leaders of the territory approached Chivington and quietly asked him to withdraw from consideration as a Republican candidate. They also apparently asked him to bow out of the campaign for statehood.

Chivington felt that much of the most vocal criticism was prompted by Confederate sympathizers— out to get even because of Chivington's success in crushing the Confederate invasion of the West two years earlier. There may have been some element of truth to that claim, given the history of the area.

Monday, January 2, 1865. General Samuel Curtis telegraphed Colonel Chivington, demanding his immediate resignation from the army. Chivington resigned his commission that day.

The dismissal of Chivington from the service was a surprising turn of events. It placated some people, but it also put the army in an interesting position; it now had no authority to punish Chivington nor even to compel him to testify at its own upcoming investigation of the Sand Creek Massacre. On the other hand, it greatly restricted Chivington's access to military records and to the testimony of officers and men he knew to be friendly to his cause.

Notes

1. Ruth Dunn, "Attack on Black Kettle's Village," Unpublished Notes, Heritage Collection, Lincoln, Nebraska Public Library, 22.
2. *The Indians*, (Time–Life Books, New York, 1973), 339.
3. Ibid., 339.
4. Ibid., 339.
5. Abbott, Leonard and McComb, *Colorado: A History of the Centennial State* (Colorado Assoc. University Press, Boulder, Colorado, 1982), 76–77.
6. David Lavender, *Bent's Fort* (University of Nebraska Press, Lincoln/London, 1972), 328.
7. *The Indians,* 340.
8. Ibid., 340.
9. Duane Shultz, *Month of the Freezing Moon* (St. Martin's Press, New York, 1990), 6.
10. David Berthrong, *The Southern Cheyennes* (University of Oklahoma Press, 1975), 221.
11. *Bent's Fort,* 384.

12. Delmot R. Oswald, "James P. Beckwourth," LeRoy R. Hafen, editor, *Trappers of the Far West* (University of Nebraska Press; Lincoln/London; 1934), 162–85.
13. Ibid., 165.
14. Carl Sifakis, *Encyclopedia of American Crime* (Facts on File, Inc., New York, 1982), 62.
15. *The Southern Cheyennes,* 162–73.
16. *Bent's Fort,* 378.
17. *Death on the Prairie,* 62.
18. Ibid., 62.
19. *The Indians,* 340.
20. Paul I. Wellman, *Death on the Prairie* (University of Nebraska Press, Lincoln/London, 1934), 63.
21. *The Southern Cheyennes*, 385–86.

–ELEVEN–

The Defense

ALTHOUGH NOT MANY PEOPLE outside Colorado would ever hear or read about it, John Chivington angrily and vehemently denied most of the charges leveled against him and his soldiers. He specifically denied that his soldiers scalped any living Indian, deliberately killed women and children, or that the attack was some sort of personal vendetta.

Notably, Chivington never denied that he personally hated the Indians, nor did he deny the possibility that some depredations were carried out by his troops. However, Chivington repeatedly pointed out that both of his bosses—Governor Evans of Colorado and General Curtis of the army—specifically ordered him to spare no Indian lives. Curtis had issued the order repeatedly. Evans had done so in person and in his public proclamations of martial law. These were the orders, said Chivington, under which he was operating and which, as an officer he was compelled to obey.

Chivington also never denied issuing orders to take no prisoners. Again, however, Chivington said he was acting under direct, public orders from the army.

It may be worth remembering that General Curtis was commander of Union troops at the Battle of Pea Ridge, Arkansas, in 1862. At Pea Ridge, warriors fighting for the Confederacy scalped and tortured wounded Union survivors. It seems possible that Curtis's frequent orders to take no Indian prisoners may have been an outgrowth of that bitter experience.

Perhaps more significantly, it was common practice at the time—in both the Civil War and the Indian wars—to order that no prisoners be taken. The simple fact is that prisoners are difficult to handle and costly to care for. Alvin Josephy, the respected historian and researcher, is among those who note that the no-prisoners command was a common order of army commanders at the time of Sand Creek.[1]

Curtis, and many others among Chivington's superiors, had been saying for several years that all Indians should be killed and no prisoners taken. Occasionally they modified the order to specify the killing of all male Indians, but most of the orders made no such distinction.

General Curtis had specifically ordered that no prisoners be taken when he sent troops to hunt for the killers of the Hungate family in June.

On June 15, Curtis ordered Chivington to crush the Indians.

On June 25, Governor Evans issued a proclamation calling on Colorado citizens to kill all hostile Indians.

On August 8, General Robert Mitchell had ordered his troops to take no prisoners while fighting Indians in northern Colorado, Wyoming, and Nebraska. No one criticized the order.

On August 12, Governor Evans specifically ordered that any Indian not "at" a fort must be killed.

On August 28, General Curtis told Chivington that the Indians "must be made to suffer."

In early November, Curtis had reprimanded and demoted Major Wynkoop for feeding Indians and accepting a partial surrender.

On November 23—barely a week before Sand Creek—General Curtis said he would accept no Indian surrender until all braves guilty of attacks against whites had either surrendered or been killed.

Throughout the summer and fall of 1864, Curtis repeatedly said that no officer may accept an Indian surrender of any kind unless Curtis personally approved it.

Also throughout that era, Curtis disallowed partial surrender—partial meaning only some members of a given tribe.

In his own defense Chivington, frequently made reference to those orders from both the army and the civilian government to which he was jointly responsible.

Chivington also pointed out that the fighting at Sand Creek was furious and confusing, and spread out over a great distance; the battlefield was over five miles long. The colonel said some of the soldiers under his command might have committed atrocities, but if so, they were out of his sight. Chivington (and many of his defenders) pointed out that Indian women and children actively participated in the battle, either by firing weapons at the soldiers or reloading the weapons for warriors who were shooting at the soldiers. Black Kettle himself testified that after his wife's shooting, he joined the women and children in loading rifles for the warriors.

Chivington repeatedly swore that he personally knew of no atrocities such as those reported by the Bent brothers, John Smith, and Jim Beckwourth. He also said that he saw no scalped or mutilated Indians on the battlefield when he walked across it after the shooting stopped. Chivington said none of those accusations were made by anyone—even the Indian survivors—until weeks after the fighting.

As to whether Black Kettle's village was really a "peace" village Chivington angrily referred to the fresh scalps found in a number of tepees, as well as bloody white man's clothing, documents, and loot from wagon trains and ranches. He again reminded everyone of General Curtis's specific orders that it was not possible for a part of a tribe to surrender; it was all or nothing.

Interestingly, the Eastern newspapers carried virtually none of these statements by Chivington. The army and Congress of his day, and many recent historians, also seem to have ignored his statements about the Sand Creek incident.

When Chivington began to realize the likelihood of his conviction by the press and in the formal hearings, he began collecting testimony from men who were actually at Sand Creek. Booted out of the army, Chivington was not allowed to present the testimony on his own behalf. However, the affidavits were later published, as were his personal notes on Sand Creek, in a book titled *To the People of Colorado: Synopsis of the Sand Creek Investigation,* published by Wagner–Camp, Denver, in June of 1865. The quotations that follow are excerpts from that book.[2]

Colonel Chivington first sought to show that the local regular army commander in the area, Major Anthony, considered the Indians on Sand Creek to be hostile:

Courtesy Colorado Historical Society

MAJOR SCOTT ANTHONY

Although under direct orders from the US Government to make sure that no Indians were allowed to surrender, Anthony issued the controversial order that Indians who gave up must camp "within sight" of Fort Lyon. It was Major Anthony who told Colonel Chivington that Black Kettle's camp contained Dog Soldiers responsible for recent murders of whites.

LT. CLARK DUNN, BEING DULY SWORN, TESTIFIED:

"I was at Fort Lyon November 28, 1864. I talked with Major Anthony in regard to the Indians in camp on Sand Creek. He said they were hostile and not under the protection of the troops; that he would have gone out himself and killed them if he had had sufficient number of troops under his command; that he stated before and after the battle of Sand Creek. In the first conversation I had with Anthony on the 28th of November, 1864, immediately after the arrival of Colonel Chivington's command, Anthony said he was 'damned glad' we had come and the only thing he was surprised at was that we had not come long before, knowing as we did how he was situated."

LT. HARRY RICHMOND, THIRD REGIMENT OF COLORADO CAVALRY, SWORN AND TESTIFIED:

"I met Major Anthony at Fort Lyon November 28, 1864. After shaking hands with me and in reply to 'where are the Indians?' asked by me, said, 'I am damned glad you have come; I have sent to Denver for assistance.' This was before the battle of Sand Creek. At another time he asserted that he should have attacked them himself if he had sufficient force. I never heard Anthony express himself except exultingly over the Battle of Sand Creek."

CAPTAIN T. G. CREE, BEING DULY SWORN, TESTIFIED:

"Major Anthony, after the battle at Sand Creek, stated that we had done a good thing in killing the Indians at Sand Creek, and believed in following it up and killing more if we could catch them."

Colonel Chivington also said that Major Anthony was fearful of Fort Lyon being overrun by the Indians camped on Sand Creek. He said the Indians had specifically threatened to attack the fort and had generally made fun of the army's ability to control them:

LT. ALEXANDER SAFELY, BEING DULY SWORN, TESTIFIED:

"I was with Colonel Chivington on November 28, 1864, when he entered Fort Lyon. I heard a conversation between Colonel Chivington and Major Anthony, then commanding Fort Lyon, both before and after the battle of Sand Creek. Major Anthony stated to Colonel Chivington, in my presence, that when he took command of Fort Lyon, or shortly afterward, he made a demand of the Indians to give up all their arms. Anthony said the Indians agreed to do it and that instead of turning in arms that were of any use to the Indians, the turned in some boys' bows and arrows and some broken double-barreled shotguns, and one Hawkins rifle that had no lock on it. He said that he then considered that they were insincere, and gave them back their arms and ordered them out of the post, saying to them that if they came back he would open up his artillery upon them. He said that they then moved from the vicinity of the post and were then on Sand Creek. He said that he was glad that we had come, as the indians had sent him word that if he, Anthony, wanted to fight he could get as big a one as he wanted by coming out to Sand Creek. Indeed, he was becoming alarmed that they would come into the post (Fort Lyon) and give him a fight. He said that he and every man that he commanded would go with Colonel Chivington's command. After the battle of Sand Creek, I heard Major Anthony say that he thought it would put a stop to the Indian War; that he considered that it was the biggest Indian fight that ever was recorded. I heard him ask Colonel Chivington for permission to visit Fort Lyon with the sick and wounded, but that he would overtake Colonel Chivington with the balance of the troops that arrived there since we left."

Colonel Chivington swore that the attack was no surprise to the Indians at Sand Creek—they were armed and ready, waiting in their carefully prepared sand pits for the assault to begin. He said it was the

Indians who fired the first shots at Sand Creek, and he sought to discredit the romanticized testimony about the death of Chief White Antelope:

LT. ALEXANDER F. SAFELY, BEING DULY SWORN, TESTIFIED:

"I witnessed the commencement of the battle of Sand Creek. I was the first man on the ground. Lt. Wilson brought his battalion up on the left of the village whilst Company H of the Third Cavalry of Colorado came up in line on the right and directly in front of the village where they was [sic]. While Lt. Wilson was coming up, I saw a man's horse running away with him, which I afterward learned was George Pierce, Company F, First Cavalry of Colorado. His horse carried him through the lower end of the village. I saw himself and the horse fall together, and shortly afterwards I saw George Pierce get up on his feet, run a short distance and stop and turn around when I saw smoke rise from an Indian's gun and also George Pierce fall.

"Immediately afterwards, Wilson's battalion commenced firing and then Company H, First Cavalry of Colorado, commenced firing. Just before Company H took its position, these Indians came out of the village toward us, firing arrows which went over Company H and took effect in a company of the Third Regiment immediately behind us. One of the Indians was killed right there.

"The next Indian that came toward us was White Antelope. He came toward us moving with a revolver in his left hand, firing at us almost at every step. In his right hand he held a bow and a number of arrows. I dismounted and shot White Antelope through the groin. He ran, and when in the creek a soldier by the name of Henderson shot him through the head."

Safely's testimony was also the first to deny that the Indians flew any flags of surrender:

"I did not at any time see any white flag in or near the Indian village. My position was such that I could have seen it had there been any waved in the village or near it by the indians."

Several men submitted sworn affidavits about the deaths of women and children at Sand Creek, and about the ferocity of the fighting there:

STEPHEN DECATUR, THIRD REGIMENT OF THE COLORADO CAVALRY, SWORN AND TESTIFIED:

"I have lived for seven years among the Indians. I was at the battle of Sand Creek. I arrived at the village at about sunrise on the morning of the 29th of November, 1864. I was acting battalion adjutant, by order of Lt. Colonel Bowen. This was my fourth battle and I never saw harder fighting on both sides. I was with Colonel Donivan's regiment in the Mexican War.

"After the battle of Sand Creek, I went over the field as clerk for Lt. Colonel Bowen to ascertain the number of dead Indians. I counted 450 warriors and do not think there were more women and children killed than would have been killed in attacking a village of whites of the same number under like circumstances. I do not think that the squaws and children that were killed could have been saved as they were in the rifle pits with the warriors who were fighting all the time most desperately. The rifle pits were dug in every place favorable for concealment or that afforded the least protection.

"After going over the field and through the village I saw things that made me feel like killing a great many more Indians. I saw men open one of a number of bundles or bales and take therefrom a number of scalps of white men, women and children. I saw one scalp in particular that had been taken entirely off the head of a white female, all the hair being with it. The hair was beautiful auburn, and very long and thick. There were two holes in the front part of the scalp. I saw a number of daguerreotypes, children's wearing apparel, and part of a lady's toilet. I saw comparatively few women and children killed, and it would have been impossible to have avoided killing them if we had tried, as they were in the rifle pits. I have seen the Lipan or Camanche [*sic*] Indians scalp their own dead to avoid having their scalps taken by whites, which may account for some of the Indians being scalped at Sand Creek.

"There was no white flag displayed by the Indians at Sand Creek; if there was, I would have seen it."

The question of whether Black Kettle's village was really a peaceful one was one of the key issues, and much of Chivington's defense testimony centered around the history and intentions of the Cheyenne warriors at Sand Creek:

DR. CALEB S. BURDSALL, SURGEON, THIRD REGIMENT, COLORADO CAVALRY, SWORN AND TESTIFIED:

"I was at the Battle of Sand Creek, fought November 29, 1864. While dressing the wounds of some soldiers in a lodge, a soldier came to the door of the lodge and asked me to look at five or six white scalps he held in his hand. One or two of these white scalps I think could not have been taken from the head more than ten days. The skin of the flesh attached to this hair was quite moist. I examined the scalp closely, my attention having been called to the fact of them having been recently taken."

STATEMENT FROM DR. T. P. BELL, SURGEON, THIRD REGIMENT, COLORADO CAVALRY, SWORN AND TESTIFIED AS FOLLOWS:

"I was at the battle of Sand Creek, fought November 29, 1864. After the battle I saw a great many white scalps in the village of the Indians at Sand Creek. I have no idea how many, though there were a great many. There were some that looked as if they might have been taken some time; others not so long, and one that I saw not over from five to eight days old at the furthest. I did not notice them particularly enough to give a more minute description, although the fresh scalp came off the head of a red-haired man."

There was also testimony which indicated that the national uproar against Chivington and the Third Colorado was part of a carefully orchestrated plot by Indian Agent Colley and several of the fur traders involved in a scheme to defraud the United States government:

> MAJOR PRESLEY TALBOT, THIRD REGIMENT, COLORADO CAVALRY, SWORN AND TESTIFIED:
> "I was at the battle of Sand Creek, fought November 29, 1864. I had a conversation with Major Anthony at Fort Lyon before the battle of Sand Creek. He expressed himself gratified that we had come to attack the Indians and said that he would have attacked them himself before if he had force enough at his command.
> "[After the battle] I had several conversations with Major Colley, Indian Agent, and John Smith, Indian Interpreter, who stated that they had considerable sympathy for me, I having been wounded in the fight, and would give me all the attention and assistance in their power, but they would do anything to damn Colonel John M. Chivington or Major Downey, that they had lost at least $6,000 by the Sand Creek fight, that they had 105 buffalo robes and two white ponies bought at the time of the attack, independent of the goods they had on the grounds, which they never had recovered, but would 'make the general government pay for the same, and damn old Chivington, eventually.'
> "John Smith had a bill made out against the general government, sworn to by one David Laudenback, which he showed to me, stating that he would go to Washington and get it allowed through the influence

of friends he had there. Smith and Colley both told me
that they were equally interested in the trade with the
Indians.

"I heard a portion of a letter read in an adjoining
room to which I lay wounded, the purport of which
was denouncing Colonel Chivington.   In the
conversation I recognized the voices of Smith, Colley,
and a man name Olmstead, all denouncing Colonel
Chivington and the Sand Creek fight. The letter was
addressed to the Superintendent of Indian Affairs,
Washington City.

"Also heard Smith in my presence boastingly say
that the eastern papers would be filled with letters
from Fort Lyon denouncing the same. Colley and
Smith stated to me that they would go in person to
Washington City and represent the Sand Creek fight
as nothing more than a massacre, and Smith said he
would realize $25,000 for his losses."

Chivington's collection of affidavits also covered the
earlier controversial battles involving Lieutenant Eayre
and Major Downing—defending them from charges that
troops under his command had ever attacked friendly
Indians or deliberately sought to harm anyone. But the
real focus of the book, of course, was self defense from
the accusations specifically related to Sand Creek.

Besides the evidence collected personally by
Chivington, other men in his command spoke out in his
defense. One such officer was Lieutenant Samuel I.
Lorah, who was Chivington's adjutant at Sand Creek.
Several years after Sand Creek Lorah wrote,

We did not go to Sand Creek to take prisoners.
Enemies of Colonel Chivington misrepresented him
for years, placing all the blame on his shoulders. If
Sand Creek was a "massacre," the men behind the
guns were responsible. I do not recall that Chivington
gave the order that aroused the rage and indignation
of the Eastern people who called us "butchers;" their
mothers and sisters had not been mistreated and slain

by the "noble" red man! Historians say he did give
such an order—but I did not carry such an order, and
I know the men did not require an order to conduct the
battle the way they did. If Chivington had given an
order to take prisoners, he would not have been
obeyed. They were all determined to give the Indians
a taste of their own medicine, to make an example and
by one stunning blow to stop the sickening atrocities
that for many months the Cheyenne, Arapaho, and
Sioux had been committing, with the emigrants and
settlers as their prey."[4]

In his own defense, Chivington stated that based on
all the evidence available to him—including statements
from the commander of Fort Lyon—he had every reason
to believe the village he attacked was hostile and
probably contained Roman Nose and many Dog
Soldiers:

"When I arrived at Fort Lyon on an expedition against
the Indians in November, 1864, I was informed that
the Indians on Sand Creek were hostile. Major
Anthony, commanding the post, whom I thought was
better acquainted than anyone else with the
relationship that existed between the Government
and the Indians as regards peace or war, informed me
on different occasions, that the Indians were hostile,
that he had repeatedly fired upon them, that the
Indians had sent him word that if he wanted a fight to
come out to Sand Creek and they would give him as
big a fight as he wanted; that every man of his
command would go gladly, and urged an immediate
departure. Anthony, after the battle of Sand Creek,
exulted over the fight and thought it was the biggest
thing on record, and witnesses say they never heard
him speak of it expect exultingly.

"The morning of the 29th day of November, 1864,
finds us before the village of the Indian foe. The first
shot is fired by them. The first man who falls is white.
No white flag is waved. None of the Indians show

signs of peace, but flying to rifle pits already prepared,
they fight with a desperation unequaled, showing
their perfect understanding of the relations that
existed as regards peace or war, as 49 killed and
wounded soldiers too plainly testifies.

"Our command consisted of nearly 600 men. The
fight continued until nearly 3 o'clock in the afternoon.
Stephen Decatur swears that being detailed as clerk,
in company with Lieutenant Colonel Bowen, he rode
over the field where the fight had occurred and
counted 450 dead warriors, that no more woman and
children were killed than would have been killed in a
white village under like circumstances, that the
women and children who were killed could not have
been saved if the troops had tried; that they were in
rifle pits with the warriors; that there were very few
women and children killed; that after he returned to
the village he saw things that made him desire to kill
more Indians; that he saw great numbers of white
scalps, daguerreotypes, part of a ladies toilet and
children's wearing apparel.

"Would not such a sight make any person feel as
Stephen Decatur did? Stephen Decatur is a husband
and a father, and how many harrowing thoughts of
murder and suffering would a spectacle like this call
up, and how many endearing reminiscences would be
swept into the gulf of horror on an occasion like this?
Stephen Decatur has spent seven years among the
Indians and is acquainted with them. He had been a
soldier before, and speaks of this fight as being the
hardest he ever saw on both sides.

"...husbands   and   fathers,   under   similar
circumstances, what would you have done? Coaxed
the chiefs to have taken their warriors away, or like
white man and true soldiers accepted their wager of
battle and whipped them if you could?

"Yet this is all that was done at Sand Creek. Though
hundreds of Colorado soldiers are today branded as
murderers and that in many instance by men without
knowing or caring whether the charge be false or true.
It is sufficient if he be a soldier, in the eyes of these
malignant   powers.   He   must,   as   a   natural

consequence, be a murderer, while others wearing the uniform of officers, without the courage to perform the brave deed themselves, are the loudest to condemn the conduct of a brother soldier who wins a single laurel that they cannot steal!

"Such men are more to be feared than the crawling viper. Perjury, larceny or robbery are no obstacle in their road to vengeance, venomous as reptiles and cowardly as curs. For what is the cause of all this trouble—whence the source of this cry of holy horror that has been run with such startling effect upon the minds of the unsophisticated people of New England, the people generally of the States, and especially the bilious old maids in the United States Senate and the House of Representatives? Why, it originates in the fertile minds of two government employees, considering together to swindle the government, as one of them states, out of $25,000. Through the influence of friends he has in Washington, and by whom he expects to get his claims allowed, probably some high official who is desirous of making an honest dollar by advocating the cause of the 'honest old men of the wilderness,' the voracious John Smith, Indian interpreter, and that reliable, respectable old gentleman, Major Colley, Indian Agent!

"But under the solemn and binding obligations of oath, what does Major Talbot say? Simply that Major Colley and John Smith stated to him that they would do anything to ruin Colonel Chivington; that they were even equally interested in their trade with the Indians—one as Indian agent, the other [as] Indian interpreter; that they had lost 105 buffalo robes and two white ponies by Colonel Chivington's attack on the Indian village at Sand Creek; that they would collect $25,000 for it of the government, and eventually damn Colonel Chivington; that John Smith boastingly stated that the Eastern newspapers would be filled with accounts of Sand Creek, as a massacre; that they would go to Washington and represent to the Committee on the Conduct of the War that Sand Creek was a massacre.

"What did they mean that they would do anything to
ruin Colonel Chivington? The word has a broad
signification, and did they not include perjury? It
appears to us without any stretch of the imagination,
they did take the expression, '...we will go to
Washington and represent Sand Creek as a
massacre!'; the eastern papers will be filled with
accounts of Sand Creek as a massacre, by letters from
Fort Lyon, and we will do anything to ruin Colonel
Chivington—draw your own conclusions!

"If it occurs to you as it does to me, perjury would be
no obstacle to these worthies in their road to
vengeance! If they would deliberately conspire to rob
the government out of $25,000 through the influence
of their friends, would they not also be guilty of
perjury to ruin their enemies, then what conclusions
are we compelled to arrive at, that perjury has been
perpetrated by these worthies, abetted by their friends
and the honorable gentlemen who encompass the
Capitol Committee on the Conduct of the War,—they
whose piercing criticism has been a terror to evil doers
in the states—they who, from their high order of
intelligence, have been supposed to be able to draw
aside the thick curtain that concealed dark deeds of
the adepts in crime and allow the sunlight of truth
and justice to shine upon it, and made the innocent
tools of two ignorant old Indian trappers and traders
to wreak disgrace and ruin upon Colonel Chivington
and Colorado soldiers generally.

"Truly these two old gentlemen, Colley and Smith,
must have read the Scriptures, for they appear to have
been in Washington, 'as innocent as lambs and as
wary as foxes.'

"Now, fellow citizens, what do you think of the
Chivington Massacre, whose horrors have filed so
many columns of the papers in the States and called
down upon Colorado so many disgraceful epithets,
while at the same time our enterprising freighters,
emigrants, and settlers, with their wives and children,
have been murdered, scalped, and their bodies
horribly mutilated by these 'much abused' sons of the
plains. The citizens of Colorado have been paying

famine prices for all they consumed; civilization retarded, and labor in our mines suspended, simply because these worthies and their friends have placed Colorado in the unenviable position of murderers, and the government would not afford the protection we so much needed, though as soon as the honorable Schuyler Colfax telegraphed the Secretary of War as to the defenseless position in which we were situated, 12,000 soldiers are immediately sent upon the plains under the gallant Connor, who will soon render the Platte route as safe for travelers as the highway of an inhabited town, unless some Indian Agent or Interpreter should have a few dollars by the attack of these troops upon some Indian village, when probably our gallant commander would be removed and a 'more humane' policy adopted.

"Lo, the poor Indian, in thy untutored greatness, you have proved yourself with the assistance of high officials, your fiends, a good diplomat. You have been a bone of contention and many a villainous swindle has been perpetrated upon the government in they name and humanity, which would put to blush the unparalleled commander of the Sons of Sin, His Satanic Majesty, The Devil."

J.M. Chivington, late colonel
First Cavalry of Colorado
Commanding District of Colorado

Notes

1. Alvin Josephy, *The Civil War in the American West* (Alfred A. Knopf, New York, 1991), 157–90.
2. John Chivington, *To the People of Colorado: Synopsis of the Sand Creek Investigation* (Wagner–Camp, Denver, June, 1865). The entire book written by Chivington, complete with the sworn testimonies quoted here, is only eighteen pages long. All of these statements, unless otherwise noted, are direct quotations from that book.
3. A daguerreotype was a crude photograph or series of photographs; the testimony presumably refers to family pictures taken from ranches or covered wagons.

4. Ruth Dunn, "Attack on Black Kettle's Village," Unpublished Notes, Heritage Collection, Lincoln, Nebraska Public Library, 17.

–TWELVE–

Unspoken Considerations

ALTHOUGH THEY WERE OVERLOOKED in the days
following the Sand Creek incident, a number of
other considerations contributed to the condemnation of John Chivington.

First, there has been a common assumption
through the years that Colonel Chivington was seeking
personal recognition and political stature by attacking
at Sand Creek; the reasoning is that he needed such
recognition because of his upcoming political campaign.
In truth, Chivington needed no additional recognition.
He was a decorated hero of the Civil War, the military
commander of Colorado, and friend of influential
Coloradans like Bill Byers. He had already virtually
sewn up the Republican nomination for Congress once
Colorado became a state, and was likely a shoo-in for the
post; it is doubtful anyone would have run against him.
One can argue that he sought political publicity to
support his drive for statehood, but the argument is
shaky, at best.

The truth is John Chivington was an enormously
popular man in Colorado. He had a charismatic

personality and charm, much in the way that John Kennedy was charismatic years later; people seemed mesmerized when he spoke and he easily won friends. His physical good looks, enhanced by his dashing dress uniforms and personal charm, caused him to be popular with the ladies of the era. His two-fisted toughness, demonstrated both in the pulpit and on the battlefield, won him the respect and admiration of the tough pioneers, miners, and frontiersmen who populated the territory.

In other words, Chivington did not need to whip a bunch of helpless Indian women and children in order to keep his name before the public. He stood to lose far more than he could gain if something went wrong with the campaign—as it ultimately did.

What happened at Sand Creek—awful as it was—was not unlike what happened scores of times before and after November 29, 1864. General Sully inflicted higher death tolls on two separate occasions following the Minnesota uprising two years earlier. Colonel Carleton's troops killed several hundred Indians—most of them women and children—in Utah two years earlier, without a complaint from Washington or the Eastern press, even though his reports boasted of shoving a hunting knife through the ear and into the brain of a captured chief.

It is also an unfortunate fact that battles which took place at Indian villages always included high tolls of women and children—simply because there were always many women and children in the villages. Some argue that the villages should not have been attacked under the circumstances. But they were attacked, regularly, by scores of different officers all over the frontier. It was only in this instance that anyone complained about it. Usually, the women and children actively participated in the defense of their villages, and scores were killed or wounded while exchanging gunfire with soldiers.

Colonel Chivington did not originate the order to take no prisoners, although the injunction is frequently cited to show what a cruel man he was. Both the army and the civilian government repeatedly issued the mandate; Chivington carried it out. One can argue that, in theory, he should have refused to obey the command on the basis of morality, but that is an entirely separate issue that was apparently never raised.

It is also obvious that there could have been battlefield atrocities at Sand Creek—such as the deliberate shooting or hurting of women and children— without Chivington's personal knowledge of such incidents. The battlefield was a huge one, and there was almost no communication during the fight. But Chivington swore repeatedly that he personally saw no such incidents.

If there were some atrocities committed by the soldiers (as there most probably were), they were committed by a group of men who, for the most part, were temporary, poorly trained volunteers. Because he was constantly on military duty away from Denver, Chivington had little time to train the men. On one occasion, General Curtis sharply criticized him for returning to Denver, even though Chivington argued that he needed the time to recruit and train the Third Colorado.

What's more, because of the personnel drain occasioned by the Civil War, the men recruited for the Third Colorado were hardly the cream of the crop. For the most part, they were out-of-work or down-on-their-luck gold miners, bar room brawlers, cowboys, and handy men—or were ranchers and homesteaders, driven from their homes by Indian raids. They were men whose families faced starvation, in part because of the attacks that shut down roads to Denver. They were desperate, frustrated, and angry civilians given a little training and much authority to get revenge for everything negative that was going on in their lives. Little wonder, then, that they seem vicious in executing their orders.

No one denied that the women and children in Black Kettle's village bore arms against the soldiers. Many persons testified that those shooting at the soldiers were of both genders and all ages. One can imagine the moral dilemma facing a soldier when he finds women and children firing rifles at him. The issue of women on the battlefield is one with which the US is still wrestling. At the time of Sand Creek it was unheard-of. That is probably one reason why Eastern newspapers expressed such revulsion at these casualties, but the very reason people who had been fighting Indians took it as a matter of course. This is not to say that deliberate cruelty to such persons is acceptable, but actual combat deaths clearly are understandable in such circumstances.

One of the enduring questions about the battle has to do with the number of Native Americans killed at Sand Creek; modern text books give the figure as anywhere from 120 to more than 500. *World Book Encyclopedia* claims a death toll of 300. Paul Wellman wrote that 300 died, 225 of which were women and children. *The American Heritage Book of Indians*[1] says 200 women and children were killed, plus seventy men and another forty or so Arapahos (without giving gender).

No one will ever know for certain how many died. At least two army officers who walked the battlefield counting the dead claimed over 450 dead warriors "and some women and children." While that is supposedly an accurate actual body count, the military—right up to "Desert Storm," the American-led UN conflict with Iraq in 1991—has habitually overstated the number of enemy dead. This was done to build the morale of one's own side while demoralizing the enemy. George Bent testified there were only 137 dead (he later raised his estimate to 167), but the Indians virtually always minimized their casualties to make the enemy think he had been less successful than he really was. In many cases, warriors claimed far fewer casualties than the number of bodies recovered by burial parties.

Possibly the most pivotal question is whether the Indians at Sand Creek were under army protection at the time of the attack—or thought they were. This is another enigma that may never be resolved. Under the orders issued by General Curtis, clearly the army considered them not to be at peace nor under army protection. Was the Cheyenne village forty miles away from Fort Lyon "at" the fort? To say so seems to stretch credibility. Additionally, Colonel Chivington himself had personally warned Black Kettle and others at the recent Denver peace conference that his orders were to kill Indians until all had surrendered.

Did the Indians themselves believe they were under army protection? There is considerable testimony indicating they did—and just as much compelling information that they suffered no such delusions.

Did the Indians fly a white flag at Sand Creek? Again, equal numbers of men on both sides of the dispute entered contradictory testimony, and the truth is simply indeterminable.

Were the Indians at Sand Creek hostile? Fresh scalps, bloody clothing, and loot taken from attacks on white targets were found throughout the village. These facts seem to indicate they were hostile, but the answer is not so simple as that. Given the generation split among Indians, it seems quite possible that the older men and women of the village—including chief Black Kettle himself—genuinely wanted to lay down their arms and live in peace. It is equally possible that the young warriors whom they admitted they could not control were continuing to attack settlers whenever and wherever they pleased, returning to the village afterwards to live in the relative safety of a peace village.

There is another enduring myth about Sand Creek; most modern text books claim that the battle at Sand Creek triggered or caused the Great Plains Indian wars. These books suggest by inference that before Sand Creek there had been no such trouble. A number of respected journals flatly state that Colonel Chivington and the Sand Creek battle were responsible for the worst wave of killings to ever hit the Great Plains.

The well-documented truth is that the year 1864, before the Sand Creek incident, was the bloodiest of the thirty-year plains Indian war. The year 1865 probably rated second in fatalities. At least a part of the blame for the extremely high bloodshed at the time was clearly because the West was largely undefended due to the Civil War, and angry war parties were free to operate with impunity throughout much of the frontier. They apparently were agitated by Confederates to make some of the attacks, which may partly explain why the trouble began easing substantially when the Civil War finally ended.

Several months after Sand Creek, General Samuel Curtis was asked whether the battle there had caused a new outburst of Indian fighting. He commented that while, "Chivington may have transgressed my field orders and otherwise acted very much against my [personal] views of propriety," his actions nonetheless did not contribute significantly to the level of hostilities and continued Indian depredations. Curtis added that no matter how much Chivington may have erred at Sand Creek, the severity of the attack and Chivington's lack of judgment, "made no new Indian enemies, but on the contrary, has reduced the number of our foes and badly frightened those who were at war against the United States."

As the whole world seemed to be unanimously against John Chivington, General Curtis once again seemed to go out of his way to relieve Chivington of some of the blame for Sand Creek. Writing to Governor Evans, Curtis said, "I abominate the extermination of women and children, [but] the popular cry of settlers and soldiers on the frontier favors an indiscriminate slaughter, which is very difficult to restrain. I abhor the style, but so it goes from Minnesota to Texas."[2]

Major Anthony, who loaned Chivington 125 army regulars and then accompanied them into battle at Sand Creek, stoutly defended Chivington and the Third Colorado. Anthony went to his grave saying that the only mistake Chivington made was in stopping too soon. Admitting that many Indians were killed there, Anthony said:

> [The battle] was a terrible one—and such a one as each of the hostile tribes on the plains richly deserve! I think one such visitation on each hostile tribe would forever put an end to Indian war on the plains, and I regret exceedingly that this punishment could not have fallen upon some other band.[3]

The battle of Sand Creek, and the uproar that ensued in its wake, clearly polarized the United States.

By late January 1865, the East was on one side of the Sand Creek issue while the West was on the other. Whether a man believed and supported John Chivington was largely dependent on where he lived. The Western consensus was pretty well summed up by a front page editorial in the *Nebraska City Press:*

WE SHOULD EXTERMINATE
THE WHOLE FRATERNITY OF RED-
SKINS![4]

The depth of the split among Americans is obvious in a formal US Congress report on the Sand Creek Massacre. The report blames John Chivington not only for Sand Creek, but for the entire Indian war, saying, in part:

> It scarcely had its parallel in the records of Indian barbarity. Fleeing women holding up their hands and praying for mercy were shot down; infants were killed and scalped in derision; men were tortured and mutilated in a way which would put to shame the savages of interior Africa.[5]

A number of respected modern journals continue to blame John Chivington alone for the nearly four decades of Indian Wars across the Great Plains. The National Geographic Society says of Sand Creek:

> No one will be astonished that a war ensued [after Sand Creek] which cost the government $30,000,000 and carried conflagration and death to the border settlements. During the spring and summer of 1865, no less than 8,000 troops were withdrawn from the effective forces engaged against the Rebellion to meet the Indian War."[6]

Another noted frontier Indian fighter, General Nelson A. Miles, wrote in his own autobiography several years later that Sand Creek was, "the foulest and most unjustifiable crime in the annals of America."[7]

The respected *American Heritage Book of Indians*[8] also blames virtually the entire plains Indian war on Sand Creek:

> Colonel Chivington took stern and instant measures; troops attacked families of the astounded Cheyennes, the Cheyennes attacked families of unsuspecting settlers, and another war was on....Black Kettle ran up both an American flag and white flag, but the boys were having too much fun. They butchered any Indian in sight.

In fact, the Great Plains Indian war started many years before Sand Creek Troops were sent to control hostile tribal groups in Wyoming and Colorado, possibly as early as 1835. Military journals and records began referring to the Plains Indian War in the middle 1840s. The final battles of the Indian war were fought in the middle 1870s, with occasional skirmishes continuing until after the turn of the century.

During the eleven months immediately preceding Sand Creek, Indian raids were extremely costly to settlers in western Kansas and eastern Colorado. One researcher says that during 1864, "savages destroyed or stole a half million dollars worth of property from the Overland Stage Company [alone]. They burned every house along the Overland line for 300 miles west of Sandy, murdered at least eighty settlers, and stole most of the stock."[9] That was along the Smoky Hill Trail, alone. Altogether, the number of settlers killed in eastern Colorado in just the warm months of 1864 may have exceeded 300.[10]

Whatever the truth may be, the army and congressional hearings both concluded that the army was to blame for a massacre at Sand Creek. The government voted to sharply increase tribal annuities the following year, including direct payments to chief Black Kettle.

Notes

1. *The American Heritage Book of Indians* (Simon & Schuster, New York, 1961), 345.
2. David Berthrong, *The Southern Cheyennes* (University of Oklahoma Press, 1975), 222.
3. Ibid., 223.
4. *The Indians* (Time–Life Books, New York, 1973), 187.
5. Official Records, United States Department of War, 1866, vol. 6, 577.
6. *The World of the American Indian* (National Geographic Society, 1964), 336.
7. Paul I. Wellman, *Death on the Prairie* (University of Nebraska Press, Lincoln/London, 1934), 65.
8. *American Heritage Book of Indians*, 345–6.
9. Floyd B. Streeter, *Prairie Trails & Cow Towns* (Devin Publications, Santa Cruz, 1963), 11.
10. *Death on the Prairie*, 60–61.

–THIRTEEN–

Epilogue

R IGHT OR WRONG, fair or unfair, Sand Creek destroyed John Chivington. Driven from the army, forced to withdraw from consideration for a political nomination, asked to stay away from the effort to win statehood for Colorado, embarrassed by months of negative national publicity, he eventually withdrew from society and left the Colorado Territory.

He went first to California, possibly hoping to start anew as a preacher or soldier there, but somehow never got started. After several months, he returned to Ohio and once again became a preacher—but that, too, was short-lived.

Chivington eventually returned to Colorado, and served for more than a decade as undersheriff of Denver county. In that position, according to one western writer, Chivington served, "with honor and fairness, and was respected by all those who worked with him."[1]

In 1874, ten years after Sand Creek, Coloradans showed their feelings toward this disgraced colonel, naming Chivington the official guest of honor at the Larimer County Fair in Fort Collins. Numerous veterans of Sand Creek and various prominent Fort Collins area businessmen and ranchers spoke at a banquet honoring Chivington, praising him warmly for his actions at Sand Creek.[2]

William Bent seemed to recover quickly from the death of his wife, Owl Woman, who died at Sand Creek. Within a few months, Bent married his wife's younger sister, Yellow Woman; such marriages were common in the Indian society.

But tragedy would not leave William Bent alone. Late in 1865, almost exactly one year after Sand Creek, Yellow Woman was killed by Pawnee scouts of the US Army. They attacked her Cheyenne village in eastern Colorado because the army believed Dog Soldiers were living there. When the battle was over, scouts found numerous scalps and loot from several recent wagon train attacks among the ruins.

In 1868, Bent married for a third time. His newest wife was Adalina Harvey, a younger white woman—but the marriage was destined to be a heart-breaker for the old trader. Adalina was an outrageous flirt, and she was attracted to men of all ages and ethnic backgrounds. About January of 1869, she vanished from Bent's Fort, apparently having run away with a young Cheyenne warrior. Bent may have known where she was, but he did not go after her, nor ever again mention her name.

In May of 1869, Bent traveled to Santa Fe, New Mexico on business. While returning to Colorado, a surprisingly heavy spring snowstorm on Raton Pass trapped his small wagon train. Bent caught the flu during the four days he spent trapped on the trail. He became increasingly ill, and was diagnosed a few days later as having pneumonia. Even though he was extremely ill and running a high fever, he insisted on pushing on toward Bent's Fort. Arriving there a week later, Bent entered the main building and collapsed. He was carried to a bed but soon lapsed into unconsciousness. Even the tender care of his oldest daughter, Mary, could not save him; William Bent died quietly on May 19, 1869.

In the wake of Sand Creek, Charles Bent became one of the most vicious of the Dog Soldiers. Although he had been attacking whites for years, and was a former Confederate soldier, Sand Creek sent him on the war path with renewed vigor. This youngest child of William Bent participated in some of the worst cases of murder, torture, kidnapping, and rape of whites over the next two years.

In 1867, Charles Bent openly split with his father, who remained loyal to the Union and a moderate in all matters. Charles decided to murder his father on the grounds that William Bent had become just like all other whites—an enemy to the Indians.

Determined to commit patricide, Charles traveled from a Dog Soldier camp near Wray, Colorado, to Bent's Fort on the Arkansas River for that specific purpose of killing his dad. By sheer coincidence, the elder Bent had gone on a business trip at the time of Charles' murderous visit.

The oldest of the Bent children, Mary, learned of the murder plot and confronted her little brother. She scolded him, then told him to leave Bent's Fort and never return; he apparently did so.

Giving up on the idea of attacking his father did not mean Charles gave up on anti–white attacks in general. He continued to lead or participate in many documented attacks for the next several months.

Ironically, it was not in a battle against the hated whites that Charles lost his life; he died as a result of battling his red brothers. In November of the year in which he tried unsuccessfully to kill his father, Charles was among the members of a Cheyenne war party that attacked a Pawnee village in extreme southern Colorado. Shot in the shoulder during the battle, Charles lost a considerable amount of blood. Other warriors rescued Charles and he was able to ride back to his own village. However, he collapsed shortly after arriving at his own tepee and died a short time later.

George Bent also became more active as a Dog Soldier in the months subsequent to Sand Creek. Over the next two years, George was active in many of the worst raids. However, he eventually grew tired of the killing and looting and decided to settle down. He went to Oklahoma and turned himself over to the authorities at a reservation set aside for the Cheyennes.

In 1872, George startled government officials by going to the authorities running the reservation and complaining that too many hostile Indians lived near him. He demanded better army protection from all the violent Indians in the area. He was moved to another reservation.

There are no additional US records pertaining to him and he presumably died on the reservation.

Roman Nose, the leader of the Dog Soldiers, carried out dozens of bloody attacks in the months following Sand Creek (just as he had for several years prior to Sand Creek). He became the object of a massive army manhunt, but managed to elude pursuing troops time after time.

He became all the more famous among a fascinated public—both Indian and white—because he was apparently impervious to injury. Roman Nose would brazenly ride up and down in front of dozens of soldiers. All of them would shoot at him, yet he was never hit. He attributed his safety to a magical bonnet given to him years before by a medicine man, who promised him that so long as he observed certain taboos, he could never be injured. His luck finally ran out as the result of technology.

In September of 1868, the army issued new seven-shot Spencer repeating rifles, and decided to use the new weapon to set a trap for Roman Nose. They armed forty men with the awesome new weapon and sent them out to look for the chief. The army correctly assumed that the Dog Soldiers would attack any group so small as forty soldiers.

Roman Nose fought his final battle in late September in extreme eastern Colorado, near the modern day town of Wray. The forty heavily armed soldiers squared off against approximately 700 Dog Soldiers on the banks of the Arikaree River. Shortly after the fighting started, the soldiers sought refuge on a small island in the middle of the mostly dry river bed. In the early moments of the fighting, Indian gunfire struck Lieutenant Frederick Beecher four times, mortally wounding him. His companions named the island (and the last battle of Roman Nose) Beecher Island.

The firepower of the forty soldiers was astounding; time after time, hundreds of warriors would attack the little group of soldiers, only to be driven away by the amazing gunfire from the repeating rifles. The Indians had been so certain of easy victory that they brought their wives and children out to watch the fighting. After

making three attacks on the island and suffering scores
of casualties, the warriors sent the women and children
back home.

Roman Nose did not participate in those initial
attacks, and his Dog Soldiers weren't sure why. After
absorbing staggering losses in the early skirmishes,
some of the warriors returned to the main village to
demand that the great leader come and lead the braves.

Roman Nose hesitated. He had a problem that he
was not eager to publicize; he had accidentally violated
the taboos of his magic war bonnet the previous evening.
One of the restrictions was that he must never eat food
prepared in a metal skillet or pan. One night earlier
Roman Nose was invited to the tepee of another warrior
for dinner. The squaw did not know about the
prohibition, and prepared dinner in a skillet stolen
earlier from a wagon train. Only after he ate did Roman
Nose realize what had happened.

Just hours later, his warriors asked him to come
and lead them into battle. Roman Nose listened
impassively to the demands of these other warriors and
made his decision. He told other tribal leaders, "I know
that I shall die." Nonetheless, he went to lead the next
charge against the Island—and was promptly shot and
killed.

The men on Beecher Island were trapped for nearly
two weeks by the constant attacks, which continued
even after Roman Nose's death. The soldiers inflicted
heavy casualties on the Dog Soldiers but were unable to
move forward or to retreat. By the third day they were
eating the flesh of their horses (killed by Indian sharpshooters early in the battle) to stay alive. The men
suffered terribly from the lack of food and from the
stench of rotting flesh; although the soldiers buried their
dead companions, they could neither bury the horses nor

the scores of dead braves whose bodies littered the ground around their island.

On two separate occasions, the badly wounded commander of the troops sent teams of two men to try to sneak through Indian lines and go for help. Although the men on the island had no way of knowing the success of these teams, both succeeded in getting through the ranks and walking more than sixty miles to get help. Finally, on the thirteenth day of the siege, responding military units rescued the surviving soldiers. The rescuers captured most of the remaining Dog Soldiers and sent them to reservations, almost ending the Dog Soldiers as a cohesive fighting unit.

Following the Sand Creek battle, Chief Black Kettle returned to life on the plains, proclaiming that he wanted only peace. Nonetheless, he participated in numerous attacks against mostly defenseless targets—ranches and covered wagon trains especially—over a period lasting several years. He helped sack and burn the town of Julesburg, and participated in a bloody attack against Fort Segwick in 1865. In striking contrast, he was simultaneously a leading spokesman for an end to the old ways and an end to conflict with whites.

After the Civil War finally ended, the army brought in its best Civil War Generals to conduct new campaigns against the hostile warriors. One of the best of those generals was the flamboyant George Armstrong Custer.

On Thanksgiving morning, November 27, 1868, four years after Sand Creek, Custer's troops attacked two large Cheyenne villages on the Washita River in Oklahoma. Custer suspected the warriors in the villages of perpetrating numerous bloody raids in Colorado, Kansas, Texas, and Oklahoma. During the fierce fighting that ensued, numerous Indians were killed—including chief Black Kettle and his wife.

Inside the tepees of the two Cheyenne villages, army search parties recovered dozens of fresh scalps, bloody clothing, and loot from ranches and wagon trains destroyed in Indian attacks.

Colorado was finally granted statehood in 1876, twelve years after the battle of Sand Creek. Virtually none of the political leaders who ruled and argued at the time of the Sand Creek incident were still in power.

Notes

1. Carl Sifakis, *Encyclopedia of American Crime* (Facts on File, Inc., New York, 1982), p 70.
2. Evadene Burris Swanson, *Fort Collins Yesterdays* (Evadene Burris Swanson, endorsed by Colorado Centennial–Bicentennial Commission, Fort Collins, Colorado, 1975), p 85.

Bibliography

Abbott, Leonard & McComb, *Colorado: A History of the Centennial State*. Boulder, Colorado: Colorado Associated University Press, 1982.

American Heritage Book of Indians. New York: Simon & Schuster, 1961.

Berthrong, David, *Southern Cheyennes*. Norman, Oklahoma: University of Oklahoma Press, 1963.

Chivington, John, *Synopsis of the Sand Creek Investigation*. Denver: Wagner–Camp, 1865.

Dunn, Ruth, "Attack on Black Kettle's Village and the Prelude to Sand Creek," The Heritage Collection, Lincoln, Nebraska Public Library.

Dunn, Ruth, "Indian Vengeance at Julesburg," The Heritage Collection, Lincoln, Nebraska Public Library.

Faust, Patricia L., *Historical Times Illustrated Encyclopedia of the Civil War*. New York: Harper & Row, 1991.

Haven, Leroy R., editor, *Trappers of the Far West*. Lincoln/London: University of Nebraska Press, 1934.

Holmes, Louis A., *Fort McPherson, Fort Cottonwood*. Lincoln, Nebraska: Johnsen Publishing Company, 1963.

Indians, The. New York: Time–Life Books, 1973.

Josephy, Alvin, *Civil War in the American West*. New York: Alfred A. Knopf, 1991.

Lavender, David, *Bent's Fort*. Lincoln/London: University of Nebraska Press, 1972

Official Records, U.S. Department of War, vol. 2, 1864.

Official Records, U.S. Department of War, vol. 6, 1866.

Rocky Mountain News, 25 June 1864.

Scott, Robert, *Glory, Glory, Glorieta*. Boulder, Colorado: Johnson Press, 1992.

Shultz, David, *Month of the Freezing Moon*. New York: St. Martin's Press, 1990.

Sifakis, Carl, *Encyclopedia of American Crime*. New York: Facts on File, Inc., 1982.

Wellman, Paul, *Death on the Prairie*. Lincoln/London: University of Nebraska Press, 1934.

World Book Encyclopedia. Chicago: World Book, Inc., 1983.

World of the American Indian. National Geographic Society, 1974.

Index

American Heritage Book of Indians; US soldiers at Sand Creek, 214

American Flag at Sand Creek, 151

Anderson, Corporal, 2–7

Anthony, Scott (Major); confronts Cheyennes on Walnut Creek, 122–3; notifies General Curtis of mass Indian surrenders, 141; denies discussing surrender with Black Kettle, 141; assigns troops to fight at Sand Creek, 143; wanted other Indian villages attacked, 228; feared Black Kettle would attack Fort Lyon, 198

Arapaho warriors linked to Hungate murders, 88

Arkansas, 8, 19, 20, 22, 27, 28, 47, 194

Army investigation of Sand Creek 139, 165–7, 169–70, 174, 178, 185, 188

attacks, by Indians: Greeley, 88 Pueblo, 88; Loveland, 88; Cheyenne Wells, 88; Julesburg, 30, 53, 90, 92, 11, 227; Fort Larned, 61, 92, 95; 114; Kelly's relay station, 93; Beaver Creek relay station, 93; Bijou relay station, 93; Santa Fe Trail, 17, 94; Limon, 94; Denver, 63, 76; Camp Collins, 94; Colorado–Kansas border, 61, 94, 101; Cow Creek relay station, 61, 96; Smoky Hill Road, 96, 218; Cimmaron Crossing, 94, 114; Beaver Creek, 101; Salina, 61, 100, 101; Plum Creek, 101, 105, 137; Smith Ranch, 101; Little Blue River, 101; Fort Kearney, 101; Liberty Station, 105; Fort Lyon, 92,107–8, 114; Fort Cottonwood, 1–10, Kettredge Ranch, 109; Little Blue relay station, 119; Overland Stage, 111;

Auraria, Colorado, visited by Horace Greeley, 42

Baiter Springs, Oklahoma, battle of, 27

Beaver Creek relay station attacked, 93

Beaver Creek, Kansas, 101